SOCIAL TRENDS IN CONTEMPORARY RUSSIA

SOCIAL TRENDS IN CONTEMPORARY RUSSIA

Also by Michael Ryan

CONTEMPORARY SOVIET SOCIETY: A Statistical Handbook
*DOCTORS AND THE STATE IN THE SOVIET UNION
THE ORGANIZATION OF SOVIET MEDICAL CARE
*SOCIAL TRENDS IN THE SOVIET UNION FROM 1950
   (*with Richard Prentice*)
THE WORK OF THE WELSH HOSPITAL BOARD, 1948–1974

*Also from the same publishers

Social Trends in Contemporary Russia

A Statistical Source-Book

Compiled and translated by

Michael Ryan
Senior Lecturer in Politics
University College of Swansea

St. Martin's Press

131153

First published in Great Britain 1993 by
THE MACMILLAN PRESS LTD
Houndmills, Basingstoke, Hampshire RG21 2XS
and London
Companies and representatives
throughout the world

A catalogue record for this book is available
from the British Library.

ISBN 0–333–56663–7

Printed in Great Britain by
Ipswich Book Co Ltd
Ipswich, Suffolk

First published in the United States of America 1993 by
Scholarly and Reference Division,
ST. MARTIN'S PRESS, INC.,
175 Fifth Avenue,
New York, N.Y. 10010

ISBN 0–312–10070–1

Library of Congress Cataloging-in-Publication Data
Ryan, Michael, 1937–
Social trends in contemporary Russia : a statistical source-book /
compiled and translated by Michael Ryan.
p.   cm.
Includes bibliographical references (p.   ) and index.
ISBN 0–312–10070–1
1. Russia (Federation)—Social conditions—Statistics.   2. Social
indicators—Russia (Federation)—Statistics.   3. Russia
(Federation)—Social policy—Statistics.   I. Title.
HN530.2.A85R9   1993
306'.0947'021—dc20   93–7913
                                                       CIP

For Jenner, Katie and Joe

Contents

Acknowledgements

I wish to express my thanks first to friends and colleagues (the categories are not mutually exclusive) who have been kind enough to take an interest in the progress of this book; my failure to mention them all by name is not to be interpreted as ingratitude. I thank David Martin for elucidating tricky passages of Russian text and Ian Jeffries, who is in the College Library before any of us, for references and photocopied material. In my own Department, Richard Taylor and Robert Bideleux have encouraged me with information and advice. I am also indebted to various members of our Library staff, especially Hazel Pember, Merlyn Brown, Ann Preece and Gwenda Bailey.

In respect of scope and detail, this book has benefited enormously due to the generous loan of materials by Mervyn Matthews of the University of Surrey. I gratefully acknowledge my indebtedness to him. As always, though, the person to whom I owe most is Ann Ryan, my dear wife.

University College of Swansea   MICHAEL RYAN

Preface

Accounts of social conditions which ignore the relevant statistical data run the risk of being compared to *Hamlet* without the Prince of Denmark. While the point applies in respect of politically stable countries, it applies with particular force to those where massive societal change has an adverse impact on everyday life. Fairly self-evidently, the second category includes contemporary Russia.

In the latter days of Communist party rule, as is well known, the policy of *glasnost* led to a very substantial improvement in the quality and range of published data about social trends and social problems throughout the former Soviet Union. Thus it became possible to obtain time-series for various highly informative indicators which, though routinely available in most countries, had been withheld from public scrutiny for reasons connected with the special character of the Soviet polity. To let one example stand for all, the figures for infant mortality ceased to appear during the 1970s when the trendline started to move in the wrong direction, presumably lest they could be interpreted as a poor reflection on the Soviet regime (which is exactly what they were).

Such suppression of the facts would be inconsistent with the principles now espoused in Boris Yeltsin's democratic Russia. It is true that, in the discontinuity and disorganisation which has followed the collapse of the Communist regime, there has been a degree of delay in the publication of standard sociographic data. What stands out most obviously, however, is the willingness of the new government to recognise the general public's right to know about even the most depressing or alarming trends. The same point applies in respect of opinion poll findings. From some of these, few people in government – and relatively few outside it – would be likely to draw comfort.

In compiling this quantitative account of selected aspects of Russian society, I have relied heavily on data collected and

published by the State Committee for Statistics for the former
USSR (Goskomstat SSSR) and, more especially, by its corresponding committee for the Russian Federation (Goskomstat
RSFSR). For example, many of the following tables present
figures which appeared first in the main series of statistical
yearbooks, *Narodnoe khozyaistvo* (*The People's Economy*). A
number of other tables take data from the census results
published by one or other Goskomstat.

Statistical information has also been gleaned from a range of
reliable secondary sources. These include the newspapers *Izvestiya* and *Argumenty i fakty* (*Arguments and Facts*).

It is relevant to point out that some of the data reported by
the latter have been obtained from the authorities in connection
with editorial responses to letters sent in by readers. For
example, a reader's letter led to publication of the disturbing
fact that there had been 1554 cases of diphtheria in the first
seven months of 1992 – an increase of 96.0 per cent over the
corresponding period in 1991.

But for another newspaper it would have been very difficult, if
not impossible, to report so fully the opinions of ordinary people
on a wide range of contemporary issues in the political,
economic and social spheres. (See Chapter 12, which collates
the results of opinion polls undertaken over the year August
1991 to August 1992, i.e. the year following the failed coup and
the consequent collapse of the Communist regime.) I refer to
Moskovskie novosti (*Moscow News*) which, in most issues,
published the findings of the latest 'Express Poll' undertaken
for it by the Centre for Public Opinion and Market Research
(VTsIOM) with the support of the Public Opinion Foundation.
In this connection I should record that I relied on the originals
and not on the English language editions. The headings are my
own, as is any commentary, unless otherwise indicated.

Although the former secrecy about politically sensitive data is
fortunately a thing of the past, there are still aspects of Russian
society about which either no information or very little is
routinely available. The distribution of income and wealth
constitutes one such. Indeed, as may be inferred from earlier
comments about sources, there is no official publication which is

directly comparable to the United Kingdom's annual compendium *Social Trends*.

Admittedly, more tabulated data could have been included here but for my decision to omit certain time-series which are known to be easily accessible in Russian sources. For example this compilation does not include any of those tables which show year-on-year increases in certain 'input' or production indicators, e.g. numbers of doctors, paramedical staff and hospital beds. My reason for this selectivity is that the trendlines serve to convey a very partial or even thoroughly misleading picture of the reality of the service in question. Incidentally, that point has been recognised by Russians themselves. It was no less than a former USSR Minister of Health who declared in 1986: 'for society today what is important is not how many there are of us [doctors] but how we work and the quality of the medical care which we provide' (*Meditsinskaya gazeta*, 1985, 5 fevralya, 5.2).

As can be seen, a number of tables give information which is broken down to the level of the major 'territorial-administrative' divisions of that vast land mass which constitutes the Russian Federation. It is an elementary but highly important point that, for a range of social indicators, the figures which refer to Russia as a whole frequently conceal substantial spatial variations. For example, in 1989 out-of-wedlock births accounted for over 30 per cent of all births in Tuva, as against 13.5 per cent for the whole of Russia. Where it has proved impossible to obtain the entire tabulation but only references to the extremes of the range, I have included the latter.

But the matter goes wider than making it possible to identify areas which report higher than average figures. For the collapse of Communist power has been followed by massive decentralisation of decision-making, especially to the homelands of ethnic minorities within the territory of what, before 1918, was accurately termed the Russian Empire.

The extreme importance of this politico-geographical development has a direct bearing on the format of this book. Thus it helps to explain why I have sought to give prominence to tabulated data and translations which help to convey the reality of a multi-ethnic state formation. It is all the more important to do so since, at present, as many as twenty homelands/republics are largely free to go their own ways. In this connection, the early placing of the contents of Chapter 2 reflects a deliberate editorial choice.

Certain categories of information, it should be said, are available as a result of questions asked in censuses, and hence are not published on an annual basis. I have included important data from the latest census, which took place in 1989, and some tables compare the 1989 data with that for earlier years in order to draw attention to significant change, or (relative) lack of change, which may be equally significant.

When he arrived back in Moscow after the abortive coup in August 1991, Mikhail Gorbachev declared that he had returned to a different country. Just how different it was at the level of high politics became increasingly apparent. All the same, as can be seen from the relevant tables, certain alarming tendencies had become strongly established well before that time. That is true, for example, of the decline in child-bearing amongst women of the most fertile age groups. Admittedly, the demographic situation can now be said to have reached crisis point; in November 1991 the number of people dying in Russia exceeded the number of births for the first time since the Second World War. Similarly, the crime statistics indicate that a degree of societal disintegration had set in substantially before the breakdown of the Communist regime. To cite one just indicator, the number of premeditated murders and attempted murders rose from 12.2 thousand to 15.6 thousand during the years 1985–90.

To say that is in no way to deny the distressing extent of social and political turmoil in Yeltsin's Russia. Here it is appropriate to refer to the results of an opinion poll carried out in August 1992. A sample of 1695 people were asked the question 'Who do you think is really in power in Russia at present?'. The largest single group of respondents (36 per cent) were simply unable to say – and not without good reason since it was far from evident who exactly was running the country.

Brief mention should be made of my editorial practice regarding the format of tables and passages of translation. In the case of certain tables I have chosen to adopt or, for presentational purposes, needed to adopt a layout which differs from that used in the source. In some cases I decided to omit the entries for certain years. I have deliberately allowed a very minor amount of replication, particularly between the tables and the passages of translated prose; this may be thought useful as providing a cross-check. Furthermore, I have amended proper names in tables so as to avoid anachronism or ensure consistency.

In a comparable way, concern for ease of reading prompted me to depart in places from an unquestioningly literal approach to translation. Furthermore, at times it has seemed desirable to omit passages from the original. It would have encumbered the text with notes to an unacceptable degree if I had drawn attention to each instance of editorial intervention.

This book was never intended to be one which integrated data from a range of countries but I thought it useful to include the small amount of cross-national information which occurred in the Russian sources. Similarly I have not commented on the accuracy of the statistics presented here, except to point out that the infant mortality figures require adjustment if they are to be strictly comparable to those of most developed countries. As a final definitional point, I should perhaps underline the fact that, unless otherwise indicated, all information relates to the Russian Federation or parts of it – and certainly not to the whole of the former USSR.

* * *

Transliterating Russian Cyrillic into the Latin alphabet presents difficulties, primarily because the former contains more symbols. A possible strategy is to simplify certain adjectival-type endings and omit the hard and soft signs. On balance, however, it seemed preferable to observe the conventions preferred by British Slavists. One example of what that entails is the use of a single diacritic comma to represent the soft sign, which indicates palatalisation of the preceding consonant. For obvious reasons, certain proper names are rendered in the form which is familiar to anglophone readers.

1 The Territorial Sub-divisions

At the time of writing, the frontiers of the country which is now known officially as the Russian Federation, or simply Russia, remain as they were before the collapse of Communist power. Moreover, with one exception, all the major 'territorial-administrative' divisions have retained their previous boundaries. Not surprisingly, though, changes of nomenclature began to occur following the emergence of powerful movements for self-government amongst the ethnic minorities of what used to be the Russian Soviet Federative Socialist Republic (RSFSR).

In the Russian Federation today there are twenty areas which have a legal right to the title of republic; these constitute historical homelands for the more numerous indigenous nationalities. Under the previous regime, with four exceptions, they were termed Autonomous Soviet Socialist Republics (ASSRs) and their existence provides the constitutional explanation for the adjective 'federative' in the title of the RSFSR. The designation of these areas constituted a sop for the centralisation of political power in Moscow: they were 'autonomous' in name but not in substance. Their current official titles, as reported by a reliable source, are given in the first table. As the footnote makes clear, in June 1992 the republic of Checheno-Ingushetiya was divided into its two constituent parts.

The number of what can most appropriately be termed regions remains at 55 – a total which has not changed since 1958. As in the past, two categories of region are identifiable in the official Russian nomenclature: the *krai* (plural: *kraya*) and the *oblast'* (plural: *oblasti*). There are 6 of the former and 49 of the latter. In certain contexts, the cities of Moscow and St. Petersburg are also classed as *oblasti* and included in tabulations on that basis.

1

As in the past, a number of regions contain territorial-administrative enclaves which were delimited mainly by reference to the residence there of the numerically smaller indigenous ethnic groups. These were referred to as autonomous *oblasti* (AO) and autonomous *okruga* (AOk). Four of the areas in question have now obtained the title of republic. Today there remain only one autonomous *oblast'* (the Jewish) and ten autonomous *okruga*. It should be said that a number of the latter have declared themselves republics, but their claim to the title has no constitutional validity.

In the list of regions a few names have not been changed in line with the reversion by their chief town or city to its pre-Revolutionary name. This is true, for example, of Leningrad *oblast'*.

As can be seen from some of the subsequent tables, the RSFSR was previously divided into eleven regions in connection with the purposes of economic planning. With the collapse of the 'administrative-command' planning of the state-owned economy and the moves towards market-driven enterprise and private ownership of property, those divisions have lost much of their previous salience.

Nomenclature of republics within the Russian Federation

Current	*Previous*
Adygeya	Adyge AO
Bashkortostan	Bashkir ASSR
Buryatiya	Buryat ASSR
Gornyi Altai (now Altai)	Gorno-Altai AO
Dagestan	Dagestan ASSR
Kabardino-Balkariya	Kabardino-Balkar ASSR
Kalmykiya-Khal'mg Tangch	Kalmyk ASSR
Karachaevo-Cherkesiya	Karachaevo-Cherkess AO
Karelia	Karelian ASSR
Komi	Komi ASSR
Marii El	Mari ASSR
Mordoviya	Mordvin ASSR
Sakha (Yakutiya)*	Yakut ASSR
North Osetiya	North Osetiya ASSR
Tatarstan	Tatar ASSR
Tuva	Tuva ASSR
Udmurtiya	Udmurt ASSR
Khakasiya	Khakass AO
Checheno-Ingushetiya	Checheno-Ingush ASSR
Chuvashiya	Chuvash ASSR

* The form Yakut-Sakha is also found.

Note: In June 1992 legislation established a separate Ingush Republic and the de facto existence of a Chechen Republic is recognised.

Source of col. 1:   *AiF*, 1992, 38–9, s. 7.

Areas and population densities of economic regions and major territorial-administrative divisions, 1991

Abbreviations: ASSR = Autonomous Soviet Socialist Republic; obl. = *oblast'*; AO = Autonomous *oblast'*; AOk = Autonomous *okrug*.

	Area in thousand km^2	Persons per $1 km^2$
Russian SFSR	**17 075.4**	**8.7**
Northern region	**1 466.3**	**4.2**
Karelian ASSR	172.4	4.6
Komi ASSR	415.9	3.0
Arkhangel'sk obl.	587.4	2.7
incl. Nenets AOk	176.7	0.3
Vologda obl.	145.7	9.3
Murmansk obl.	144.9	8.0
North-west region	**196.5**	**42.3**
St. Petersburg (Leningrad) and Leningrad obl.	85.9	78.1
Novgorod obl.	55.3	13.6
Pskov obl.	55.3	15.3
Central region	**485.1**	**62.8**
Bryansk obl.	34.9	42.0
Vladimir obl.	29.0	57.2
Ivanovo obl.	23.9	55.1
Tver' (Kalinin) obl.	84.1	19.9
Kaluga obl.	29.9	36.1
Kostroma obl.	60.1	13.5
Moscow and Moscow obl.	47.0	334.5
Orel obl.	24.7	36.5
Ryazan' obl.	39.6	34.1
Smolensk obl.	49.8	23.4
Tula obl.	25.7	72.2
Yaroslavl' obl.	36.4	40.5

Volgo-Vyatka region	**263.3**	**32.2**
Mari ASSR	23.2	32.7
Mordvin ASSR	26.2	36.8
Chuvash ASSR	18.3	73.6
Nizhnii Novgorod (Gor'kii) obl.	74.8	49.6
Kirov obl.	120.8	14.1
Central Black-earth region	**167.7**	**46.3**
Belgorod obl.	27.1	51.7
Voronezh obl.	52.4	47.2
Kursk obl.	29.8	44.8
Lipetsk obl.	24.1	51.2
Tambov obl.	34.3	38.3
Volga region	**536.4**	**30.9**
Kalmyk ASSR	76.1	4.3
Tatar ASSR	68.0	54.1
Astrakhan' obl.	44.1	22.8
Volgograd obl.	113.9	23.1
Samara (Kuibyshev) obl.	53.6	27.0
Penza obl.	43.2	35.0
Saratov obl.	100.2	27.0
Ul'yanovsk obl.	37.3	38.3
North Caucasus region	**355.1**	**48.0**
Dagestan ASSR	50.3	36.9
Kabardino-Balkar ASSR	12.5	62.2
North Osetiya ASSR	8.0	80.3
Checheno-Ingush ASSR	19.3	67.7
Krasnodar krai	83.6	61.9
incl. Adyge AO	7.6	57.6
Stavropol krai	80.6	36.3
incl. Karachaevo-Cherkess AO	14.1	30.3
Rostov obl.	100.8	43.1
Ural' region	**824.0**	**24.8**
Bashkir ASSR	143.6	27.7
Udmurt ASSR	42.1	38.7
Kurgan obl.	71.0	15.6

	Area in thousand km^2	Persons per $1\,km^2$
Ural' region (*cont.*)		
Orenburg obl.	124.0	17.7
Perm' obl.	160.6	19.4
incl. Komi-Permyak AOk	32.9	4.9
Sverdlovsk obl.	194.8	24.3
Chelyabinsk obl.	87.9	41.4
West Siberia region	**2 427.2**	**6.2**
Altai krai	261.7	10.9
incl. Gorno-Altai AO	92.6	2.1
Kemerovo obl.	95.5	33.3
Novosibirsk obl.	178.2	15.7
Omsk obl.	139.7	15.5
Tomsk obl.	316.9	3.2
Tyumen' obl.	1 435.2	2.2
incl. Khanty-Mansi AOk	523.1	2.5
and Yamalo-Nenets AOk	750.3	0.7
East Siberia region	**4 122.8**	**2.2**
Buryat ASSR	351.3	3.0
Tuva ASSR	170.5	1.8
Krasnoyarsk krai	2 401.6	1.5
incl. Khakass AO	61.9	9.3
and Taimyr		
(Dolgano-Nenets) AOk	862.1	0.1
and Evenki AOk	767.6	0.03
Irkutsk obl.	767.9	3.7
incl. Ust'-Ordynskii		
Buryat AOk	22.4	6.2
Chita obl.	431.5	3.2
incl. Aginskii-Buryat AOk	19.0	4.1
Far East region	**6 215.9**	**1.3**
Yakut ASSR	3 103.2	0.4
Primor'e krai	165.9	13.9

Khabarovsk krai	824.6	2.2
incl. Jewish AO	36.0	6.1
Amur obl.	363.7	3.0
Kamchatka obl.	472.3	1.0
incl. Koryak AOk	301.5	0.1
Magadan obl.	1 199.1	0.4
incl. Chukot AOk	737.7	0.2
Sakhalin obl.	87.1	8.2
Kaliningrad obl.	15.1	58.7

Source: *Nar. khoz. RSFSR 1990*, s. 77–80.

Notes:

(1) Former city/*oblast'* names are given in brackets.

(2) In the interest of clarity, the adjectival forms of area names used in the source have been rendered as proper nouns wherever appropriate. For example, I give *Amur*, not *Amurskaya*, and *Nizhnii Novgorod*, not *Nizhegorodskaya* (that variant of the city's name exists only in adjectival form).

Population of major territorial-administrative divisions, 1991 (thousands)

	Total	Urban	Rural	Urban as %	Rural as %
RSFSR	**148 543**	**109 799**	**38 744**	**73.9**	**26.1**
Republics					
Bashkir	3 984	2 574	1 410	64.6	35.4
Buryat	1 056	635	421	60.2	39.8
Dagestan	1 854	816	1 038	44.0	56.0
Kabardino-Balkar	777	478	299	61.5	38.5
Kalmyk	328	151	177	46.0	54.0
Karelian	799	655	144	82.0	18.0
Komi	1 265	961	304	76.0	24.0
Mari	758	470	288	62.0	38.0
Mordvin	964	556	408	57.7	42.3
North Osetiya	643	443	200	68.9	31.1
Tatar	3 679	2 716	963	73.8	26.2
Tuva	307	146	161	47.5	52.5
Udmurt	1 628	1 145	483	70.3	29.7
Checheno-Ingush	1 307	598	709	45.8	54.2
Chuvash	1 346	800	546	59.4	40.6
Yakut	1 109	738	371	66.6	33.4
Kraya					
Altai	2 851	1 601	1 250	56.1	43.9
Krasnodar	5 175	2 817	2 358	54.4	45.6
Krasnoyarsk	3 625	2 641	984	72.9	27.1
Primor'e	2 299	1 784	515	77.6	22.4
Stavropol'	2 926	1 573	1 353	53.8	46.2
Khabarovsk	1 851	1 462	389	79.0	21.0
Oblasti					
Amur	1 074	730	344	67.9	32.1
Arkhangel'sk	1 577	1 164	413	73.8	26.2
Astrakhan'	1 007	685	322	68.0	32.0
Belgorod	1 401	897	504	64.0	36.0

Bryansk	1 464	1 000	464	68.3	31.7
Vladimir	1 660	1 322	338	79.7	20.3
Volgograd	2 632	1 998	634	75.9	24.1
Vologda	1 361	898	463	66.0	34.0
Voronezh	2 475	1 523	952	61.6	38.4
Ivanovo	1 317	1 076	241	81.7	18.3
Irkutsk	2 863	2 314	549	80.8	19.2
Kaliningrad	887	701	186	79.0	21.0
Kaluga	1 080	759	321	70.3	29.7
Kamchatka	473	384	89	81.3	18.7
Kemerovo	3 180	2 780	400	87.4	12.6
Kirov	1 700	1 202	498	70.7	29.3
Kostroma	813	560	253	68.9	31.1
Kurgan	1 110	612	498	55.1	44.9
Kursk	1 336	792	544	59.3	40.7
St. Petersburg*					
(Leningrad)	5 035	5 035	—	100	—
Leningrad *oblast'*	1 670	1 103	567	66.1	33.9
Lipetsk	1 234	784	450	63.5	36.5
Magadan	534	436	98	81.6	18.4
Moscow*	9 003	9 002	1	99.99	0.01
Moscow *oblast'*	6 718	5 339	1 379	79.5	20.5
Murmansk	1 159	1 068	91	92.1	7.9
Nizhnii Novgorod					
(Gor'kii)	3 712	2 874	838	77.4	22.6
Novgorod	755	530	225	70.2	29.8
Novosibirsk	2 796	2 098	698	75.1	24.9
Omsk	2 163	1 475	688	68.2	31.8
Orenburg	2 194	1 432	762	65.3	34.7
Orel	901	566	335	62.8	37.2
Penza	1 512	948	564	62.7	37.3
Perm'	3 110	2 411	699	77.5	22.5
Pskov	845	540	305	63.9	36.1
Rostov	4 348	3 098	1 250	71.2	28.8
Ryazan'	1 349	899	450	66.6	33.4
Samara (Kuibyshev)	3 290	2 669	621	81.1	18.9

| | Total | Urban | Rural | Urban | Rural |
				as %	
Saratov	2 708	2 026	682	74.8	25.2
Sakhalin	717	612	105	85.3	14.7
Sverdlovsk	4 730	4 135	595	87.4	12.6
Smolensk	1 166	802	364	68.8	31.2
Tambov	1 315	751	564	51.7	42.9
Tver' (Kalinin)	1 676	1 203	473	71.8	28.2
Tomsk	1 012	696	316	68.8	31.2
Tula	1 855	1 512	343	81.5	18.5
Tyumen'	3 156	2 440	716	77.3	22.7
Ul'yanov	1 430	1 032	398	72.2	27.8
Chelyabinsk	3 641	3 001	640	82.4	17.6
Chita	1 392	916	476	65.8	34.2
Yaroslavl'	1 476	1 209	267	81.9	18.1

* Includes outlying settlements which are administratively subordinate to the city.

Source: *Nar. khoz. SSSR 1990*, s. 68–70.

Note: Former city/*oblast'* names are given in brackets. [The population figures given above are estimates for 1 January. Ed.]

Population of autonomous *oblasti* and autonomous *okruga*, 1991
(thousands)

	Total	Urban	Rural
Nenets AOk	55	34	21
Adyge AO	437	230	207
Karachaevo-Cherkess AO	427	211	216
Komi-Permyak AO	160	48	112
Gorno-Altai AO	196	53	143
Khanty-Mansi AOk	1314	1201	113
Yamalo-Nenets AOk	493	407	86
Khakass AO	577	419	158
Taimyr (Dolgano-Nenets) AOk	54	36	18
Evenki AOk	25	7	18
Ust'-Ordynskii Buryat AOk	138	26	112
Aginskii-Buryat AOk	78	26	52
Jewish AO	220	145	75
Koryak AOk	40	15	25
Chukot AOk	154	111	43

Source: *Nar. khoz. RSFSR 1990*, s. 77–80.

2 A Multi-ethnic Federation

Indigenous peoples of RSFSR who have their own homeland,*
at 1989 census

Key to columns:
1 Percentage of population of RSFSR
2 Percentage resident in their own homeland
3 Number resident elsewhere in RSFSR
(thousands)

	1	2	3
Total	**100**		
Russians	**81.5**		
Others with homeland in RSFSR	**12.0**	**55.2**	**7943**
Tatars	3.8	32.0	3757
Peoples of Dagestan	1.2	82.6	304
Avars	0.4	91.2	48
Dargwa	0.2	79.4	73
Kumyks	0.2	83.6	45
Lezghi	0.2	79.4	53
Lakk	0.1	86.3	14
Tabasarans	0.06	83.6	16
Nogais	0.05	38.4	46
Rutuls	0.01	76.7	4.5
Tsakhurs	0.01	80.0	1.3
Aguls	0.004	77.8	3.9
Chuvash	1.2	51.1	867
Bashkirs	0.9	64.2	481
Mordvinians	0.7	29.2	760
Chechens	0.6	81.7	164

Udmurts	0.5	69.5	218
Mariitsy	0.4	50.4	320
Ossetes	0.3	83.2	67
Buryats	0.3	81.7	76
Kabarda	0.3	94.2	23
Yakuts	0.3	96.1	15
Komi	0.2	86.7	44
Ingush	0.1	76.1	51
Tuvinians	0.1	93.6	7.7
Kalmyks	0.1	88.2	20
Karelians	0.1	63.2	46
Balkardians	0.05	90.4	7.5
Adyge	0.1	77.7	28
Karachais	0.1	86.1	21
Cherkess	0.03	79.3	11
Altais	0.05	85.2	10
Khakass	0.05	80.1	16
Jews	0.4	1.7	528
Komi-Permyaki	0.1	64.8	52
Nentsy	0.02	87.1	3.5
Evenki	0.02	11.6	26
Khanty	0.02	53.4	10
Mansi	0.01	79.3	1.7
Chukchi	0.01	78.9	3.2
Koryaki	0.01	73.5	2.3
Dolgany	0.004	75.0	1.7

* Russian: *natsional'no-territorial' noe obrazovanie*.

Source: *Nar. khoz. RSFSR 1990*, s. 89–90.

Note: Some of the names of small ethnic groups are simply trans-literated from the Russian original; in most cases the *i* or *y* endings indicate the plural form. [Ed.]

Ethnic Russians in the RSFSR at postwar censuses

	Thousands	*As % of total population*
1959	97 863	83.3
1970	107 747	82.8
1979	113 522	82.6
1989	119 873	81.5

Source: *AiF*, 1992, 38–9, s. 7.

Further nationalities in RSFSR, at 1989 census

Key to columns:　1　Percentage of population of RSFSR
　　　　　　　　　2　Number in RSFSR as percentage of the
　　　　　　　　　　　nationality in former USSR

	1	2
Indigenous nationalities of former USSR Republics	**5.3**	**6.9**
Ukrainians	3.0	9.9
Belorussians	0.8	12.0
Uzbeks	0.1	0.8
Kazakhs	0.4	7.8
Georgians	0.1	3.3
Azeris	0.2	5.0
Lithuanians	0.05	2.3
Moldavians	0.01	5.2
Latvians	0.03	3.2
Kirgiz	0.03	1.7
Tadziks	0.03	0.9
Armenians	0.4	11.5
Turkmenians	0.03	1.5
Estonians	0.03	4.5
Nationalities living in RSFSR who do not have their own homelands* in it	**0.2**	**23.1**
Abazin	0.02	98.1
Abkhaz	0.0	6.9
Aleuts	0.0	91.7
Veps	0.01	97.1
Gagauz	0.01	5.1
Mountain Jews	0.01	60.9
Georgian Jews	0.0	7.3
Central Asian Jews	0.0	3.9
Izhora	0.0	54.8
Itel'meny	0.0	97.9
Karaites	0.0	26.1

	1	2
Nationalities living in RSFSR who do not have their own homelands* in it (*cont.*)		
Karakalpaks	0.0	1.5
Kety	0.0	97.4
Krymchaki	0.0	23.3
Livs	0.0	28.3
Nanaitsy	0.01	98.8
Nganasany	0.0	98.7
Negidal'tsy	0.0	94.4
Nivkhi	0.0	99.1
Oroki	0.0	94.2
Orochi	0.0	96.5
Saami	0.0	97.1
Sel'kupy	0.0	98.7
Talysh	0.0	0.9
Crimean Tatars	0.01	7.8
Tats	0.01	63.3
Tofalary	0.0	98.8
Udin	0.0	13.8
Udegeitsy	0.0	94.6
Ul'chi	0.0	98.1
Gipsies	0.1	58.4
Chuvantsy	0.0	91.6
Shors	0.01	94.6
Eveny	0.01	99.2
Entsy	0.0	94.7
Eskimos	0.0	99.1
Yukaghiry	0.0	97.4

* Russian: *Natsional'noe obrazovanie*.

Note: 0.0 indicates an insignificant number.

Source: *Nar. khoz. RSFSR 1990*, s. 91–2.

Ethnic composition of the population, 1979 and 1989; and percentage for whom their mother tongue was either that of their ethnic group or Russian, at 1989 census

| Nationality | Thousands | | Mother tongue (%) | |
	1979	1989	Ethnic	Russian
Total	**137 410**	**147 022**	**94.6**	**5.1**
Russians	113 522	119 866	99.95	99.95
Tatars	5 006	5 522	85.6	14.2
Ukrainians	3 658	4 363	42.9	57.0
Chuvash	1 690	1 774	77.5	22.3
Bashkirs	1 291	1 345	72.8	10.1
Belorussians	1 052	1 206	36.2	63.5
Mordvinians	1 111	1 073	69.0	30.9
Chechens	712	899	98.8	1.1
Germans	791	842	41.8	58.0
Udmurts	686	715	70.8	29.0
Mariitsy	600	644	81.9	17.8
Kazakhs	518	636	87.9	11.5
Avars	438	544	97.8	1.6
Jews	692	537	8.9	90.5
Armenians	365	532	67.8	31.9
Buryats	350	417	86.6	13.3
Ossetes	352	402	93.2	6.4
Kabarda	319	386	97.6	2.2
Yakuts	326	380	94.0	5.9
Dargwa	280	353	98.0	1.5
Komi	320	336	71.0	28.9
Azeris	152	336	84.2	14.6
Kumyks	226	277	97.7	1.8
Lezghi	203	257	94.0	4.5
Ingush	166	215	98.2	1.6
Tuvinians	165	206	98.6	1.4
Peoples of the North	156	182	52.5	36.3
Nentsy	29	34	77.7	17.6
Evenki	27	30	30.4	28.3
Khanty	21	22	60.8	38.5
Eveny	12	17	43.8	27.4

Nationality	Thousands		Mother tongue (%)	
	1979	*1989*	*Ethnic*	*Russian*
Peoples of the North (cont.)				
Chukchi	14	15	70.4	28.3
Nanaitsy	10	12	44.1	55.3
Koryaki	7.6	8.9	52.4	46.8
Mansi	7.4	8.3	36.7	62.7
Dolgany	4.9	6.6	84.0	15.4
Nivkhi	4.4	4.6	23.3	76.2
Sel'kupy	3.5	3.6	47.7	50.6
Ul'chi	2.5	3.2	30.7	66.5
Itel'meny	1.3	2.4	18.8	80.2
Udegeitsy	1.4	1.9	24.3	68.1
Saami	1.8	1.8	42.0	56.8
Eskimos	1.5	1.7	51.6	45.9
Chuvantsy*	—	1.4	18.5	71.1
Nganasany	0.8	1.3	83.4	15.3
Yukaghiry	0.8	1.1	32.0	45.9
Kety	1.1	1.1	48.8	49.4
Orochi	1.0	0.9	17.8	81.0
Tofalary	0.6	0.7	42.8	55.6
Aleuts	0.5	0.6	25.3	72.2
Negidal'tsy	0.5	0.6	26.6	69.5
Entsy**	—	0.2	46.5	37.9
Oroki***	—	0.2	44.7	54.2
Moldavians	102	173	66.8	31.7
Kalmyks	140	166	93.1	6.9
Gipsies	121	153	85.8	12.6
Karachais	126	150	97.8	2.1
Komi-Permyaki	146	147	71.7	28.7
Georgians	89	131	70.5	28.6
Uzbeks	72	127	79.6	18.1
Karelians	133	125	48.6	51.2
Adyge	107	123	95.3	4.6
Koreans	98	107	36.5	63.1
Lakk	91	106	95.1	3.9
Poles	100	95	15.1	74.7
Tabasaran	73	94	96.7	2.4

Greeks	70	92	44.5	52.3
Khakass	69	79	76.7	23.1
Balkars	62	78	95.3	4.2
Nogais	59	74	90.4	2.9
Lithuanians	67	70	59.6	39.6
Altais	59	69	85.1	14.8
Cherkess	49	51	91.6	5.2
Finns	56	47	36.2	63.1
Latvians	67	47	42.8	56.6
Estonians	56	46	41.5	58.1
Kirghiz	15	42	89.5	8.9
Turkmenians	23	40	86.5	11.8
Tadzhiks	18	38	80.1	17.4
Abazin	29	33	94.0	4.3
Bulgarians	25	33	44.9	53.5
Crimean Tatars	5.2	21	89.4	9.7
Rutuls	15	20	95.5	3.1
Tats	13	19	83.5	14.4
Aguls	12	18	95.5	3.4
Shors	15	16	57.5	40.9
Veps	7.6	12	51.3	48.3
Mountain Jews	6.5	11	75.2	21.1
Gagauz	4.2	10	63.9	31.9
Turks	3.6	9.9	85.6	10.0
Assyrians	8.7	9.6	49.5	48.8
Abkhaz	4.1	7.2	65.7	29.6
Tsakhurs	4.8	6.5	95.0	3.2
Karakalpaks	1.7	6.2	73.9	22.4
Rumanians	3.8	6.0	46.5	36.0
Hungarians	4.3	5.7	61.2	35.1
Chinese	5.7	5.2	30.8	67.2
Kurds	1.6	4.7	80.5	12.6
Czechs	4.5	4.4	35.4	62.6
Arabs	2.3	2.7	76.0	16.2
Uighurs	1.7	2.6	59.3	32.6
Persians	1.7	2.6	42.3	38.8
Vietnamese	0.7	2.1	98.0	1.8
Khalkha-Mongols	1.8	2.1	88.5	9.7
Spanish	2.0	2.1	50.8	48.0

| Nationality | Thousands | | Mother tongue (%) | |
	1979	1989	Ethnic	Russian
Serbs	0.8	1.6	44.1	29.7
Cubans	1.2	1.6	71.5	14.4
Central Asian Jews	0.3	1.4	18.0	79.8
Georgian Jews	0.1	1.2	62.8	34.0
Udins	0.2	1.1	70.6	24.8
Afghans	0.2	0.9	67.3	19.8
Slovaks	0.4	0.7	57.2	35.9
Karaites	0.9	0.7	10.7	87.7
Dungans	1.2	0.6	65.8	28.5
Italians	0.4	0.6	51.5	47.8
Japanese	0.7	0.6	46.5	49.9
Peoples of India and Pakistan	0.2	0.5	61.1	29.5
Croatians	0.1	0.5	51.4	47.4
Dutch	0.4	0.5	27.7	66.1
Izhora	0.4	0.4	41.9	56.6
French	0.3	0.4	56.0	40.1
Krymchaki	1.4	0.3	29.3	68.6
Albanians	0.2	0.3	43.6	54.7
Belu	0.04	0.3	46.5	45.1
Austrians	0.3	0.3	29.5	59.7
English	0.1	0.2	64.6	34.5
Talysh	0.002	0.2	66.8	23.3
Americans	0.1	0.2	69.7	20.6
Livs	0.003	0.1	48.4	43.7
Others	3.6	19.0	9.5	5.5

* In 1979 Chuvantsy were included with Chukchi. ** In 1979 Entsy were included with Nenets. *** In 1979 Oroki were included in the grouping 'Others'.

Note: The territory of the RSFSR contains over 120 different 'nationalities and peoples' (*natsional'nostei i narodov*). Among the indigenous peoples of Russia the following have had the highest rates of population growth: Ingush, Chechens, the peoples of Dagestan, Tuvinians, Kabarda, Karachais, Buryats, Kalmyks, Altais, the peoples of the North and Yakuts.

The reduction in the numbers of Mordvinians, Karelians and Jews is explained by ethnic assimilation, and also by emigration and natural loss in the case of the Jews.

The majority of the population in Russia regard the language of their own ethnic group as their mother tongue. The proportion of such persons, however, has declined slightly since 1979 among all indigenous nationalities except Bashkirs.

Definitional notes:

(1) For 'mother tongue' the source gives a third category, namely 'other languages'. In respect of the total population this residual is 0.3 per cent.

(2) Ethnic and linguistic affiliation as reported in the censuses are determined by the respondents themselves, or by parents in the case of children.

Source: *Nar. khoz. RSFSR 1989*, s. 74–7.

More numerous nationalities of autonomous areas of RSFSR, at 1989 census

	Numbers	*Percentages*
Bashkir ASSR	3 943 113	**100**
Bashkirs	863 808	21.9
Russians	1 548 291	39.3
Tatars	1 120 702	28.4
Chuvash	118 509	3.0
Mariitsy	105 768	2.7
Ukrainians	74 990	1.9
Mordvinians	31 923	0.8
Udmurts	23 696	0.6
Buryat ASSR	1 038 252	**100**
Buryats	249 525	24.0
Russians	726 165	70.0
Ukrainians	22 868	2.2
Tatars	10 496	1.0
Dagestan ASSR	1 802 188	**100**
Avars	496 077	27.5
Dargwa	280 431	15.6
Kumyks	231 805	12.9
Lezghi	204 370	11.3
Lakk	91 682	5.1
Tabasaran	78 196	4.3
Nogais	28 294	1.6
Rutuls	14 955	0.8
Aguls	13 791	0.8
Tsakhurs	5 194	0.3
Russians	165 940	9.2
Azeris	75 463	4.2
Chechens	57 877	3.2
Kabardino-Balkar ASSR	753 531	**100**
Kabarda	363 494	48.2
Balkars	70 793	9.4

Russians	240 750	32.0
Ukrainians	12 826	1.7
Kalmyk ASSR	**322 579**	**100**
Kalmyks	146 316	45.4
Russians	121 531	37.7
Darghwa	12 878	4.0
Karelian ASSR	**790 150**	**100**
Karelians	78 928	10.0
Russians	581 571	73.6
Belorussians	55 530	7.0
Ukrainians	28 242	3.6
Finns	18 420	2.3
Komi ASSR	**1 250 847**	**100**
Komi	291 542	23.3
Komi-Permyaki	1 076	0.1
Russians	721 780	57.7
Ukrainians	104 170	8.3
Belorussians	26 730	2.1
Tatars	25 980	2.1
Germans	12 866	1.0
Chuvash	11 253	0.9
Mari ASSR	**749 332**	**100**
Mariitsy	324 349	43.3
Russians	355 973	47.5
Tatars	43 850	5.9
Chuvash	8 993	1.2
Mordvin ASSR	**963 504**	**100**
Mordvinians	313 420	32.5
Russians	586 147	60.8
Tatars	47 328	4.9
North Osetiya ASSR	**632 428**	**100**
Ossetes	334 876	53.0
Russians	189 159	29.9
Ingush	32 783	5.2

	Numbers	*Percentages*
North Osetiya ASSR (*cont.*)		
Armenians	13 619	2.2
Georgians	12 284	1.9
Ukrainians	10 088	1.6
Tatar ASSR	**3 641 742**	**100**
Tatars	1 765 404	48.5
Russians	1 575 361	43.3
Chuvash	134 221	3.7
Ukrainians	32 822	0.9
Mordvinian	28 859	0.8
Udmurts	24 796	0.7
Mariitsy	19 446	0.5
Bashkirs	19 106	0.5
Tuva ASSR	**308 557**	**100**
Tuvinians	198 448	64.3
Russians	98 831	32.0
Udmurt ASSR	**1 605 663**	**100**
Udmurts	496 522	30.9
Russians	945 216	58.9
Tatars	110 490	6.9
Ukrainians	14 167	0.9
Checheno-Ingush ASSR	**1 270 429**	**100**
Chechens	734 501	57.8
Ingush	163 762	12.9
Russians	293 771	23.1
Armenians	14 824	1.2
Ukrainians	12 637	1.0
Chuvash ASSR	**1 338 023**	**100**
Chuvash	906 922	67.8
Russians	357 120	26.7
Tatars	35 689	2.7
Mordvinians	18 686	1.4

Yakut ASSR	**1 094 065**	**100**
Yakuts	365 236	33.4
Russians	550 263	50.3
Ukrainians	77 114	7.0
Tatars	17 478	1.6
Evenki	14 428	1.3
Eveny	8 668	0.8
Adyge AO	**432 046**	**100**
Adyge	95 439	22.1
Russians	293 640	68.0
Ukrainians	13 755	3.2
Armenians	10 460	2.4
Gorno-Altai AO	**190 831**	**100**
Altais	59 130	31.0
Russians	115 188	60.4
Kazakhs	10 692	5.6
Jewish AO	**214 085**	**100**
Jews	8 887	4.2
Russians	178 087	83.2
Ukrainians	15 921	7.4
Karachaevo-Cherkess AO	**414 970**	**100**
Karachais	129 449	31.2
Cherkess	40 241	9.7
Russians	175 931	42.4
Abazin	27 475	6.6
Nogais	12 993	3.2
Khakass AO	**566 861**	**100**
Khakass	62 859	11.1
Russians	450 430	79.5
Ukrainians	13 223	2.3
Germans	11 250	2.0
Aginskii-Buryat AOk	**77 188**	**100**
Buryats	42 362	54.9
Russians	31 473	40.8

	Numbers	Percentages
Komi-Permyak AOk	**158 526**	**100**
Komi-Permyaki	95 415	60.2
Russians	57 272	36.1
Koryak AOk	**39 940**	**100**
Koryaki	6 572	16.4
Chukchi	1 460	3.6
Itel'meny	1 179	3.0
Eveny	713	1.8
Russians	24 773	62.0
Ukrainians	2 896	7.2
Nenets AOk	**53 912**	**100**
Nentsy	6 423	11.9
Russians	35 489	65.8
Komi	5 124	9.5
Taimyr (Dolgano-Nenets) AOk	**55 803**	**100**
Dolgany	4 939	8.8
Nenets	2 446	4.4
Russians	37 438	67.1
Ust'-Ordynskii Buryat AOk	**135 870**	**100**
Buryats	49 298	36.3
Russians	76 827	56.5
Tatars	4 391	3.2
Khanty-Mansi AOk	**1 282 396**	**100**
Khanty	11 892	0.9
Mansi	6 562	0.5
Nentsy	1 144	0.1
Russians	850 297	66.3
Ukrainians	148 317	11.6
Tatars	97 689	7.6
Bashkirs	31 151	2.4
Belorussians	27 775	2.2

Chukot AOk	**163 934**	**100**
Chukchi	11 914	7.3
Eskimos	1 452	0.9
Eveny	1 336	0.8
Russians	108 297	66.1
Ukrainians	27 600	16.8
Evenki AOk	**24 769**	**100**
Evenki	3 480	14.0
Russians	16 718	67.5
Yamalo-Nenets AOk	**494 844**	**100**
Nentsy	20 917	4.2
Khanty	7 247	1.5
Sel'kupy	1 530	0.3
Russians	292 808	59.2
Ukrainians	85 022	17.2
Tatars	26 431	5.3
Belorussians	12 609	2.6

Source: *Nar. khoz. RSFSR 1989*, s. 80–5.

Percentage of main nationalities of autonomous areas in non-manual and manual employment, at censuses of 1979 and 1989*

	Non-manual**		*Manual***	
	1979	*1989*	*1979*	*1989*
RSFSR	**31.2**	**35.1**	**68.8**	**64.9**
Russians	32.1	35.9	67.9	64.1
Bashkir ASSR	**26.5**	**30.9**	**73.5**	**69.1**
Bashkirs	21.1	27.8	78.9	72.2
Russians	31.3	34.2	68.7	65.8
Buryat ASSR	**29.4**	**34.6**	**70.6**	**65.4**
Buryats	36.3	43.0	63.7	57.0
Russians	27.8	31.8	72.2	68.2
Dagestan ASSR	**25.3**	**28.9**	**74.7**	**71.1**
Avars	20.3	24.3	79.7	75.7
Dargwa	17.1	21.8	82.9	78.2
Kumyks	26.1	31.1	73.9	68.9
Lakk	33.6	38.0	66.4	62.0
Lezghi	24.3	28.8	75.7	71.2
Tabasaran	16.9	23.4	83.1	76.6
Russians	40.6	43.0	59.4	57.0
Kabardino-Balkar ASSR	**28.8**	**32.9**	**71.2**	**67.1**
Kabarda	23.4	30.2	76.6	69.8
Balkars	26.9	31.2	73.1	68.8
Russians	34.4	36.5	65.6	63.5
Kalmyk ASSR	**28.8**	**34.0**	**71.2**	**66.0**
Kalmyks	31.2	38.8	68.8	61.2
Russians	32.4	35.7	67.6	64.3
Karelian ASSR	**29.4**	**32.9**	**70.6**	**67.1**
Karelians	23.5	27.0	76.5	73.0
Russians	32.6	35.1	67.4	64.9

Komi ASSR	**28.0**	**30.9**	**72.0**	**69.1**
Komi	27.3	29.5	72.7	70.5
Russians	30.1	32.9	69.9	67.1
Mari ASSR	**27.5**	**31.2**	**72.5**	**68.8**
Mariitsy	16.7	32.2	83.3	77.8
Russians	36.8	38.9	63.2	61.1
Mordvin ASSR	**25.3**	**30.3**	**74.7**	**69.7**
Mordvinians	19.2	26.6	80.8	73.4
Russians	29.1	33.0	70.9	67.0
North Osetiya ASSR	**32.7**	**35.8**	**67.3**	**64.2**
Ossetes	32.0	36.3	68.0	63.7
Russians	35.9	37.8	64.1	62.2
Tatar ASSR	**27.7**	**32.5**	**72.3**	**67.5**
Tatars	23.3	29.7	76.7	70.3
Russians	32.7	36.3	67.3	63.7
Tuva ASSR	**27.2**	**32.8**	**72.8**	**67.2**
Tuvinians	19.0	27.2	81.0	72.8
Russians	36.3	41.0	63.7	59.0
Udmurt ASSR	**28.0**	**32.0**	**72.0**	**68.0**
Udmurts	19.1	24.7	80.9	75.3
Russians	33.1	36.1	66.9	63.9
Checheno-Ingush ASSR	**24.3**	**29.7**	**75.7**	**70.3**
Chechens	14.0	21.8	86.0	78.2
Ingush	19.6	28.3	80.4	71.7
Russians	38.6	43.2	61.4	56.8
Chuvash ASSR	**23.9**	**28.3**	**76.1**	**71.7**
Chuvash	19.4	24.8	80.6	75.2
Russians	35.2	37.6	64.8	62.4
Yakut ASSR	**33.2**	**34.1**	**66.8**	**65.9**
Yakuts	33.3	36.1	66.7	63.9
Russians	34.4	34.7	65.6	65.3

	Non-manual**		Manual**	
	1979	1989	1979	1989
Adyge AO	**27.3**	**32.3**	**72.7**	**67.7**
Adyge	31.1	38.6	68.9	61.4
Russians	26.2	30.7	73.8	69.3
Gorno-Altai AO	**27.2**	**31.8**	**72.8**	**68.2**
Altais	21.2	29.1	78.8	70.9
Russians	29.6	33.3	70.4	66.7
Jewish AO	**29.0**	**33.6**	**71.0**	**66.4**
Jews	45.0	49.1	55.0	50.9
Russians	28.2	33.2	71.8	66.8
Karachaevo-Cherkess AO	**26.1**	**30.8**	**73.9**	**69.2**
Karachais	21.9	26.9	78.1	73.1
Cherkess	26.0	31.2	74.0	68.8
Russians	28.8	32.9	71.2	67.1
Khakass AO	**26.1**	**29.9**	**73.9**	**70.1**
Khakass	20.9	27.6	79.1	72.4
Russians	27.3	31.1	72.7	68.9
Aginskii-Buryat AOk	**25.7**	**31.6**	**74.3**	**68.4**
Buryats	31.3	37.3	68.7	62.7
Russians	21.7	25.2	78.3	74.8
Komi-Permyak AOk	**23.7**	**28.2**	**76.3**	**71.8**
Komi-Permyaki	21.2	26.7	78.8	73.3
Russians	28.6	31.2	71.4	68.8
Koryak AOk	**35.7**	**35.4**	**64.3**	**64.6**
Koryaki	12.0	16.6	88.0	83.4
Russians	40.6	39.2	59.4	60.8
Nenets AOk	**30.1**	**33.3**	**69.9**	**66.7**
Nentsy	14.6	17.3	85.4	82.7
Russians	32.7	35.9	67.3	64.1

Taimyr (Dolgano-Nenets) AOk	**32.3**	**33.7**	**67.7**	**66.3**
Dolgany	17.3	23.0	82.7	77.0
Nenets	7.3	12.5	92.7	87.5
Russians	35.9	36.1	64.1	63.9
Ust'-Ordynskii Buryat AOk	**24.0**	**28.5**	**76.0**	**71.5**
Buryats	33.4	39.3	66.6	60.7
Russians	20.1	22.9	79.9	77.1
Khanty-Mansi AOk	**28.6**	**32.3**	**71.4**	**67.7**
Khanty	16.9	21.6	83.1	78.4
Mansi	20.0	22.7	80.0	77.3
Russians	30.8	35.2	69.2	64.8
Chukot AOk	**34.8**	**35.8**	**65.2**	**64.2**
Chukchi	12.2	15.7	87.8	84.3
Russians	37.6	38.4	62.4	61.6
Evenki AOk	**34.1**	**36.0**	**65.9**	**64.0**
Evenki	22.0	26.7	78.0	73.3
Russians	37.4	38.1	62.6	61.9
Yamalo-Nenets AOk	**28.7**	**34.0**	**71.3**	**66.0**
Nentsy	6.4	12.4	93.6	87.6
Russians	33.4	37.6	66.6	62.4

* Based on responses to a census question put to 25 per cent of the population.
** Predominant form of employment.

Source: *Statisticheskii Press-byulleten'* 1992, 1, s. 121–6.

Managers (directors) from titular ethnic group as percentage of all managers in productive sectors* of economies of ASSRs, 1 January 1989

ASSR	Ethnic group	As % of pop. in ASSR	As % of managers
Bashkir	Bashkirs	21.9	24.2
Buryat	Buryats	24.0	36.7
Dagestan	Peoples of ASSR	79.3	83.8
Kabardino-Balkar	Titular peoples	57.6	69.8
Kalmyk	Kalmyks	45.3	48.1
Karelian	Karelians	9.9	9.0
Komi	Komi	23.3	18.3
Mari	Mariitsy	43.3	26.4
Mordvin	Mordvinians	32.5	37.9
North Osetiya	Ossetes	52.9	75.5
Tatar	Tatars	48.5	64.1
Tuva	Tuvinians	64.3	39.6
Udmurt	Udmurts	30.9	30.8
Checheno-Ingush	Titular peoples	70.7	71.5
Chuvash	Chuvash	67.8	59.2
Yakut	Yakuts	33.4	38.2

* Includes: industry, agriculture, transport, communications and construction. See: *AiF*, 1989, 2, s. 5.

Source: *Nar. khoz. RSFSR 1989*, s. 118.

3   The Growth of Towns

Urban and rural population, 1959–91

	Total (millions)	Urban	Rural	Urban (as percentage)	Rural (as percentage)
1959	117.5	61.6	55.9	52	48
1970	130.1	81.0	49.1	62	38
1979	137.6	95.4	42.2	69	31
1989	147.4	108.4	39.0	74	26
1990	148.0	109.2	38.8	74	26
1991	148.5	109.8	38.7	74	26

Source: *Nar. khoz. RSFSR 1990*, s. 76.

Number of towns and urban-type settlements, 1959–91

	Total	Towns	Urban-type settlements
1959	2372	877	1495
1970	2838	969	1869
1979	3045	999	2046
1989	3230	1037	2193
1991	3256	1052	2204

Sources: *Gorodskie poseleniya RSFSR*, s. 5; *Nar. khoz. RSFSR 1990*, s. 85.

Distribution of towns by size of population, 1979 and 1991

| Category | Number | | Population (millions) | |
(thousands)	1979	1991	1979	1991
Up to 3	7	7	0.01	0.01
3–4.9	22	16	0.1	0.1
5–9.9	90	80	0.7	0.6
10–19.9	242	250	3.5	3.7
20–49.9	348	365	10.9	11.8
50–99.9	138	166	9.3	11.3
100–249.9	86	88	13.0	13.0
250–499.9	40	46	13.8	15.9
500–999.9	18	21	12.7	13.3
Over 1 million	8	13	18.9	26.3
Total	**999**	**1 052**	**82.9**	**96.0**

Note: More than a third of the population live in towns with a population of over half a million.

Source: *Nar. khoz. RSFSR 1990*, s. 85.

Distribution of urban-type settlements by size of population, 1979 and 1991

| Category | Number | | Population (millions) | |
(thousands)	1979	1991	1979	1991
Up to 3	530	614	1.0	1.1
3–4.9	568	517	2.2	2.0
5–9.9	655	714	4.5	5.0
10–19.9	262	324	3.4	4.3
20–49.9	31	35	0.9	0.9
Total	**2046**	**2204**	**12.0**	**13.3**

Source: *Nar. khoz. RSFSR 1990*, s. 85.

**Distribution of rural population centres by size of population,
1979 and 1991**

Category	Number (thousands)		Population (thousands)	
	1979	*1991*	*1979*	*1991*
Up to 50	78.5	74.8	1 606	1 304
51–100	26.3	18.1	1 899	1 312
101–200	24.1	17.9	3 498	2 595
201–500	27.0	22.2	8 605	7 116
501–1 000	12.5	11.5	8 746	8 087
1 001–2 000	6.0	5.7	8 084	7 759
2 001–3 000	1.3	1.3	3 056	3 060
Over 3 000	1.3	1.4	6 974	7 830
Total	**177.0**	**152.9**	**42 468**	**39 063**
		As percentages		
Up to 50	44.3	49.0	3.8	3.3
51–100	14.9	11.8	4.5	3.4
101–200	13.6	11.7	8.2	6.7
201–500	15.3	14.5	20.3	18.2
501–1 000	7.1	7.5	20.6	20.7
1 001–2 000	3.4	3.8	19.0	19.9
2 001–3 000	0.7	0.8	7.2	7.8
Over 3 000	0.7	0.9	16.4	20.0
Total	**100**	**100**	**100**	**100**

Note: In 1989 the number of rural population centres (*punktov*) was 24 000 less than in 1979, mainly on account of abolition or amalgamation; over this period 14 400 were abolished and 2 000 were amalgamated. At the 1989 census there were no more than ten inhabitants in every fifth settlement (*poselenie*) as against every seventh centre in 1979.

Source: *Nar. khoz. RSFSR 1989*, s. 67.

Towns and urban-type settlements: by economic regions and major territorial-administrative divisions, 1991

	Towns	Urban-type settlements
Russian SFSR	**1052**	**2204**
Northern region	**62**	**165**
Karelian ASSR	13	44
Komi ASSR	10	47
Arkhangel'sk	13	39
incl. Nenets AOk	1	2
Vologda obl.	15	14
Murmansk obl.	11	21
North-west region	**60**	**92**
St Petersburg (Leningrad)*	9	17
Leningrad obl.	27	40
Novgorod	10	22
Pskov obl.	14	13
Central region	**244**	**410**
Bryansk obl.	16	31
Valdimir obl.	21	36
Ivanovo obl.	17	32
Tver' (Kalinin) obl.	23	31
Kaluga obl.	17	15
Kostroma obl.	11	19
Moscow*	2	4
Moscow obl.	72	109
Orel obl.	7	14
Ryazan' obl.	12	28
Smolensk obl.	15	16
Tula obl.	21	50
Yaroslavl' obl.	10	25
Volgo-Vyatka region	**63**	**173**
Mari ASSR	4	19
Mordvin ASSR	7	19

Chuvash ASSR	9	8
Nizhnii Novgorod (Gor'kii) obl.	25	69
Kirov obl.	18	58
Central Black-earth region	**50**	**87**
Belgorod obl.	9	22
Voronezh obl.	15	22
Kursk obl.	10	24
Lipetsk obl.	8	6
Tambov obl.	8	13
Volga region	**90**	**184**
Kalmyk ASSR	3	6
Tatar ASSR	19	24
Astrakhan' obl.	5	14
Volgograd obl.	19	32
Samara (Kuibyshev) obl.	11	24
Penza obl.	10	16
Saratov obl.	17	36
Ul'yanovsk obl.	6	32
North Caucasus region	**103**	**117**
Dagestan ASSR	10	14
Kabardino-Balkar ASSR	7	9
North Osetiya ASSR	6	7
Checheno-Ingush ASSR	7	4
Krasnodar krai	28	29
incl. Adyge AO	2	5
Stavropol krai	22	18
incl. Karachaevo-Cherkess AO	4	11
Rostov obl.	23	36
Ural' region	**141**	**281**
Bashkir ASSR	18	43
Udmurt ASSR	6	16
Kurgan obl.	9	6
Orenburg obl.	12	25
Perm' obl.	25	57
incl. Komi-Permyak AOk	1	3
Sverdlovsk obl.	44	100
Chelyabinsk obl.	27	34

	Towns	Urban-type settlements
West Siberia region	80	194
Altai krai	12	33
incl. Gorno-Altai AO	1	2
Kemerovo obl.	20	47
Novosibirsk obl.	14	20
Omsk obl.	6	25
Tomsk obl.	5	16
Tyumen' obl.	23	53
incl. Khanty-Mansi AOk	12	27
and Yamalo-Nenets AOk	6	9
East Siberia region	71	207
Buryat ASSR	6	31
Tuva ASSR	5	3
Krasnoyarsk krai	28	62
incl. Khakass AO	5	18
and Taimyr		
(Dolgano-Nenets) AOk	1	1
and Evenki AOk	0	1
Irkutsk obl.	22	64
incl. Ust'-Ordynskii		
Buryat AOk	0	4
Chita obl.	10	47
incl. Aginskii-Buryat AOk	0	4
Far East region	66	289
Yakut ASSR	11	67
Primor'e krai	11	46
Khabarovsk krai	9	44
incl. Jewish AO	2	12
Amur obl.	9	33
Kamchatka obl.	3	11
incl. Koryak AOk	0	5

Magadan obl.	4	52
incl. Chukot AOk	2	18
Sakhalin obl.	19	36
Kaliningrad obl.	22	5

* Includes outlying settlements which are administratively subordinate to the city.

Source: *Nar. khoz. RSFSR 1990*, s. 5–8.

Population of towns with over 100 000 inhabitants, 1979–91
(thousands)

(For ease of reference, names are listed in the order of the Latin alphabet.)

	1979	1989	1991
Abakan	128	154	157
Al'met'evsk	110	129	133
Angarsk	239	266	269
Anzhero-Sudzhensk	105	108	107
Arzamas	93	109	112
Armavir	162	161	162
Arkhangel'sk	385	416	420
Astrakhan'	461	509	512
Achinsk	117	122	122
Balakovo	152	197	201
Balashikha	118	136	138
Barnaul	535	602	607
Belgorod	240	300	311
Berezniki	185	201	200
Biisk	212	233	235
Blagoveshchensk			
(Amur *oblast'*)	172	206	211
Bratsk	214	256	259
Bryansk	394	452	459
Cheboksary	308	420	436
Chelyabinsk	1030	1142	1148
Cherepovets	266	310	316
Cherkessk	91	113	117
Chita	303	366	376
Dzerzhinsk	257	285	287
Dimitrovgrad	106	124	127
Ekaterinburg (Sverdlovsk)	1211	1367	1375
Elektrostal'	139	152	153

Elets	112	120	121
Engel's	161	181	184
Glazov	81	104	106
Groznyi	375	400	401
Ivanovo	465	481	482
Izhevsk	549	635	647
Irkutsk	550	626	641
Ioshkar-Ola	201	242	248
Kazan'	993	1094	1105
Kaliningrad	355	401	408
Kaliningrad			
(Moscow *oblast'*)	133	159	162
Kaluga	265	311	316
Kamensk-Ural'skii	187	208	209
Kamyshin	112	122	124
Kansk	101	110	110
Kemerovo	462	520	521
Khabarovsk	528	601	613
Khimki	118	133	136
Kineshma	101	105	105
Kirov	421	478	491
Kiselevsk	122	128	127
Kislovodsk	101	114	117
Kovrov	143	160	162
Kolomna	147	162	164
Kolpino	114	141	145
Komsomol'sk-na-Amur	264	315	319
Kostroma	255	278	282
Krasnodar	560	621	631
Krasnoyarsk	796	913	924
Kuznetsk	94	99	100
Kurgan	310	356	364
Kursk	375	424	433
Leninsk-Kuznetskii	132	134	133
Lipetsk	396	450	460
Lyubertsy	154	165	165

	1979	*1989*	*1991*
Magadan	121	152	155
Magnitogorsk	406	440	444
Maikop	128	149	153
Makhachkala	251	317	334
Mezhdurechensk	91	107	108
Miass	150	168	170
Michurinsk	101	109	109
Moscow	8142	8972	9003
less outlying popn. under city soviet	7935	8774	8801
Murmansk	381	468	473
Murom	114	124	126
Mytishchi	141	154	154
Naberezhnie Chelny (Brezhnev)	301	500	510
Nal'chik	207	235	241
Nakhodka	133	160	165
Nevinnomyssk	104	121	123
Neftekamsk	70	107	111
Nizhnevartovsk	109	241	247
Nizhnekamsk	134	191	196
Nizhnii Novgorod (Gor'kii)	1344	1438	1445
Nizhnii Tagil	398	440	439
Novgorod	186	229	234
Novokuznetsk	541	600	602
Novokuibyshevsk	109	113	113
Novomoskovsk (Tula *oblast'*)	147	146	146
Novorossiisk	159	186	189
Novosibirsk	1312	1437	1446
Novotroitsk	95	106	108
Novocheboksarsk	85	115	119
Novocherkassk	183	188	189
Novoshakhtinsk	104	108	107
Noginsk	119	123	123
Noril'sk	180	175	169

Obninsk	73	100	104
Odintsovo	101	125	128
Oktyabr'skii	88	105	107
Omsk	1014	1148	1167
Orel	305	337	345
Orenburg	458	547	557
Orekhovo-Zuevo	132	137	137
Orsk	246	271	272
Penza	483	543	551
Pervoural'sk	129	142	144
Perm'	999	1091	1100
Petrozavodsk	234	269	277
Petropavlovsk-Kamchatskii	215	269	273
Podol'sk	202	209	209
Prokop'evsk	266	274	273
Pskov	176	204	208
Pyatigorsk	110	129	131
Rostov-na-Donu	934	1019	1028
Rubtsovsk	157	172	173
Rybinsk (Andropov)	239	251	253
Ryazan'	453	515	527
Salavat	137	150	151
Samara (Kuibyshev)	1206	1254	1257
Saransk	263	312	320
Sarapul	107	110	111
Saratov	856	905	911
Sergiev Posad (Zagorsk)	107	115	116
Sverdlovsk	1211	1365	1375
Severodvinsk	197	249	252
Serov	101	104	104
Serpukhov	140	141	141
Shakhty	209	226	228
Shchelkovo	100	109	110
Smolensk	299	341	350
Solikamsk	101	110	110
Sochi	287	337	342

	1979	1989	1991
St. Petersburg (Leningrad)	4588	5024	5035
less outlying popn.			
under city soviet	4073	4460	4467
Stavropol'	258	318	328
Staryi Oskol	115	174	182
Sterlitamak	220	247	252
Surgut	107	248	261
Syzran'	166	174	175
Syktyvkar	171	220	224
Taganrog	276	292	294
Tambov	270	305	310
Tver' (Kalinin)	412	451	455
Tol'yatti	502	631	655
Tomsk	421	502	506
Tula	514	540	544
Tyumen'	359	477	494
Ulan-Ude	300	353	362
Ul'yanovsk	464	625	648
Usol'e-Sibirskoe	103	106	107
Ussuriisk	147	158	160
Ust'-Ilimsk	69	109	112
Ufa	978	1078	1097
Ukhta	87	111	112
Velikie Luki	102	114	115
Vladivostok	550	634	648
Vladikavkaz (Ordzhonikidze)	279	300	306
Vladimir	296	350	356
Volgograd	929	999	1007
Volgodonsk	91	176	181
Volzhskii	209	269	278
Vologda	237	283	289
Vorkuta	100	116	117
Voronezh	783	887	900
Votkinsk	90	104	105

Yakutsk	152	187	193
Yaroslavl'	597	633	638
Yuzhno-Sakhalinsk	140	159	164
Zelenograd	140	158	163
Zhukovskii	90	101	101
Zlatoust	198	208	208

Sources: *Nar. khoz. RSFSR 1990*, s. 81–4; *AiF*, 1991, 35, s. 8.

Number of persons migrating between town and country, 1989–91

	1989	*1990*	*1991*
To towns	1 212 496	1 051 529	847 000
To the country	883 385	839 155	802 000
Balance	−329 111	−212 374	−45 000

Note: After a long period of large-scale migration from rural areas to the towns, in recent years a persisting reduction has occurred; people have been attracted to the land, where at present income is higher and food is closer to hand.

Source: *AiF*, 1992, 41, s. 6.

4 The Demographic Crisis

Number of births, 1980–90

	Total number (thousands)	To mothers who had borne 3 or more	
		Number (thousands)	% of all births
1980	2203	263	12
1985	2375	385	16
1986	2486	442	18
1987	2500	459	18
1988	2348	422	18
1989	2161	368	17
1990	1989	323	16

Source: *Nar. khoz. RSFSR 1990*, s. 102.

Number of births to women under age 20, 1989

Total		To mothers aged:				Total as % of all births
	Under 16	16	17	18	19	
255 766	1 850	10 421	34 269	78 446	130 780	11.8
			Urban areas			
175 929	1 035	6 618	22 812	53 549	91 915	11.6
			Rural areas			
79 837	815	3 803	11 457	24 897	38 865	12.5

Source: *Demograficheskii ezhegodnik SSSR 1990*, s. 318–19.

Births per 1000 women of specifed age groups, 1989

Ages	Total	Urban	Rural
15–49*	**59.8**	**54.0**	**80.6**
Under 20**	52.5	45.6	78.8
20–24	163.9	149.1	212.2
25–29	103.1	96.4	124.8
30–34	54.6	50.5	68.9
35–39	22.0	19.5	31.9
40–44	5.0	4.1	9.0
45–49	0.2	0.1	0.3
Total fertility rate			
	2.016	1.829	2.697
Net reproduction rate			
	0.953	0.866	1.267

* Also includes births to women under 15 and over 50.
** Calculation uses number of women in age group 15–19.

Source: *Demograficheskii ezhegodnik SSSR 1990*, s. 308, 634.

Note: The total fertility rate gives the number of children who would be born per woman if the age-specific fertility rates of the year in question were to apply throughout the child-bearing period.

The net reproduction rate measures the extent to which women are replacing themselves by having daughters who may be expected to survive to the age at which their mothers gave birth to them. Thus it takes account of both fertility and mortality. A value of 1.00 for this rate indicates that replacement level obtains. [Ed.]

Out-of-wedlock births* as percentage of all births, 1980–90

Year	As % of: Total births	Urban	Rural
1980	10.8	9.6	13.4
1985	12.0	11.3	13.6
1986	12.4	11.8	13.9
1987	12.7	12.0	14.5
1988	13.0	12.1	15.1
1989	13.5	12.6	15.6
1990	14.6	13.8	16.5

* Births to women not in registered marriage.

Note: The number of children born outwith registered marriage stood at 291 000 in 1990, as against 238 000 in 1980.

Source: *Nar. khoz. RSFSR 1989*, s. 100.

Number of out-of-wedlock births,* 1989

Total*	Number registered by mother**	Col. 2 as % of col. 1
291 725	168 110	57.6
	Urban areas	
191 824	120 052	62.6
	Rural areas	
99 901	48 058	48.1

* Births to women not in registered marriage.
** The residual represents births registered jointly by the mother and father.
Source of cols. 1 and 2:   *Demograficheskii ezhegodnik SSSR 1990*, s. 316–17, 634.

Spatial variation in out-of-wedlock births, 1989

The proportion of children born out of wedlock was significantly higher than the average for Russia as a whole in Tuva (over 30 per cent in 1989) and also in Kalmykiya, North Osetiya, Checheno-Ingushetiya, Buryatiya, Yakutiya, Krasnoyarsk and Primor'e *kraya* and Perm', Irkutsk, Chita, Amur and Sakhalin *oblasti*. In those territories the indicator ranged from 23 to 17 per cent of all births.

A noticeable increase has occurred in the extent of out-of-wedlock births among young women under the age of 20 years. In 1989 the number of such births was over 50 000, a rate of 10 per 1000 women of this age group. By comparison the figures for 1979 were, respectively, 48 000 and 8 per 1000 women of this age group.

Source: *Vestnik statistiki*, 1991, 7, s. 21.

Distribution of birth rates by administrative territories, 1986–90

Number of births per	Number of territories				
1000 population	1986	1987	1988	1989	1990
less than 14	3	2	12	31	45
14.0–15.9	19	24	28	21	17
16.0–17.9	24	20	15	12	4
18.0–19.9	15	15	10	2	3
20 and over	12	12	8	7	4

Notes: In recent years a substantial decline in child-bearing amongst women of the most fertile age groups, combined with a reduction in their numbers of almost a million over 1988–90, has led to a sharp fall in the birth rate. In 1990 the rate was 20 per cent lower than in 1987 and there were half a million fewer births.

In 1990 amongst the 73 administrative territories a fairly high birth rate was maintained only in Dagestan (26.0 births per 1000 population), Tuva (25.9), Checheno-Ingushetiya (24.6), Kalmykiya (20.7), Kabardino-Balkariya (19.9), Yakutiya (19.6) and Buryatiya (18.3).

In 1990 the total fertility rate for Russia as a whole was 2.1. In Moscow and Leningrad, however, and in Murmansk, Leningrad, Ivanovo, Moscow, Tula, Yaroslav, Samara, and Kamchatka regions, it did not exceed 1.55–1.84.

The birth rate of ethnic Russians, who comprised 81.5 per cent of the population at the time of the 1989 census, is lower than that of other major nationalities within the Federation. In 1989 rates per 1000 population for selected ethnic groups were as follows:

Russians	13.4
Ukrainians	18.1
Belorusssians	18.1
Armenians	18.3
Germans	19.3
Tatars	25.2
Azeris	27.3

Source: *Vestnik statistiki*, 1991, 7, s. 20–1.

Births, deaths and natural increase per 1000 population, 1980–91

Year	Total	Urban	Rural
		Births	
1980	15.9	15.8	16.1
1985	16.6	16.1	17.8
1986	17.2	16.7	18.6
1987	17.2	16.6	18.6
1988	16.0	15.4	17.6
1989	14.6	14.0	16.4
1990	13.4	12.7	15.5
1991	12.2		
		Deaths	
1980	11.0	10.0	13.4
1985	11.3	10.3	14.0
1986	10.4	9.6	12.5
1987	10.5	9.7	12.7
1988	10.7	9.9	13.0
1989	10.7	10.0	12.7
1990	11.2	10.4	13.3
1991	11.3		
		Natural increase	
1980	4.9	5.8	2.7
1985	5.3	5.8	3.8
1986	6.8	7.1	6.1
1987	6.7	6.9	5.9
1988	5.3	5.5	4.6
1989	3.9	4.0	3.7
1990	2.2	2.3	2.2
1991	0.9		

Sources: *Nar. khoz. RSFSR 1990*, s. 98; *Kratkii statisticheskii byulleten' 1991*, s. 6.

Balance of migratory flows between the RSFSR and former USSR republics, 1989–91 (thousands in 1990)

	1989	1990 *(thousands)*	1991
Ukrainian SSR	2056	−4.2	−66075
Belorussian SSR	−4565	23.3	4654
Uzbek SSR	41602	65.9	35873
Kazakh SSR	43930	54.5	29526
Georgian SSR	10802	14.5	28748
Azerbaidzhanian SSR	37693	52.0	20736
Lithuanian SSR	1136	5.0	4379
Moldavian SSR	1951	1.0	2502
Latvian SSR	546	3.9	5838
Kirgiz SSR	4958	21.2	17745
Tadzhik SSR	6698	40.3	17559
Armenian SSR	8603	1.4	4064
Turkmen SSR	4631	5.2	4501
Estonian SSR	582	4.3	4164

Note: During the three years in question Russia had a negative balance of migration only with the Ukrainian and Belorussian republics, i.e. more people moved to those republics from Russia in the years indicated than left them for Russia. With the other republics Russia had a positive balance of migration. It should be recognised that many different nationalities were represented amongst the migrants.

Source: *AiF*, 1992, 38–9, s. 7.

The population is declining

During the past five years the birth rate in Russia has fallen by 30 per cent. In November of 1991 the number of people who died in the republic exceeded the number of births for the first time since the Second World War. The difference was 4000 and in December it had risen to 12000; in January 1992 it was 19700. The gap between births and deaths continued to widen in February and March. The State Committee for Statistics envisages a reduction in the number of inhabitants as a consequence of negative natural increase in 43 areas of Russia; more than two-thirds of the population are resident there.

The situation is particularly serious in large and environmentally polluted cities. Amongst children in the first year of life there has been an increase in the number of diseases linked to inadequate diet. The most widespread are the same as were common in the wartime and post-war generations – serious rickets, diatheses and other allergic dermatoses, stunted growth, disorders in the functioning of the gastro-intestinal system, and obesity. Even according to the official statistics, which ignore many symptoms previously categorised as diseases, only about a third of all new-born infants remain healthy up to their first birthday. Statistical data show that, starting in 1989, the mortality rate among new-borns has ceased to fall. In January 1992 the mortality rate among children under the age of one year was 9 per cent higher than in January 1991.

According to the forecast of the State Committee for Statistics, the birth rate will decline further by 9–10 per cent during the course of 1992. This apparently absolutely natural reaction of society to the socio-economic and political crisis could have more serious consequences than the hypothetical threat of civil war.

Source: Article by I. Demchenko in *Izvestiya*, 1992, 30 marta, s. 2.

Towards the end of 1991 the number of births fell below the number of deaths. The negative natural increase led to a decline in the population of 64 000 over the period from November 1991 to May 1992. While in 1988–90 the negative natural increase occurred mainly in the *oblasti* of the North-West, Central and Central Black-earth zones, in 1991–2 it had extended to the *oblasti* of the Volga area, Krasnodar and Altai *kraya*, Rostov, Sverdlovsk, Kemerovo and Kaliningrad *oblasti*, Karelia, Mordoviya and Adygeya. In May 1992 there were 42 regions, in which two-thirds of the population live, where the number of deaths outstripped the number of births.

Source: *Ekonomika i zhizn'*, 1992, 30, s. 5.

Births, deaths and natural increase per 1000 population: all ethnic groups and Russians, 1979 and 1989

	Births		Deaths		Natural increase	
	1979	*1989*	*1979*	*1989*	*1979*	*1989*
All	15.8	14.6	10.8	10.7	5.0	3.9
Russians	15.0	13.4	10.9	10.9	4.1	2.5
Urban areas						
All	15.7	14.0	9.8	10.0	5.9	4.0
Russians	15.3	13.2	9.8	10.1	5.5	3.1
Rural areas						
All	16.1	16.4	13.1	12.7	3.0	3.7
Russians	14.2	13.8	13.8	13.7	0.4	0.1

Source: *Demograficheskii ezhegodnik SSSR 1990*, s. 184, 186–7.

Births, deaths and natural increase in economic regions and major territorial-administrative divisions per 1000 population, 1990

	Births	*Deaths*	*Natural increase*
Russian SFSR	13.4	11.2	2.2
Northern region	13.0	9.1	3.9
Karelian ASSR	13.2	10.1	3.1
Komi ASSR	13.4	7.4	6.0
Arkhangel'sk obl.	13.5	9.8	3.7
incl. Nenets AOk	16.7	7.0	9.7
Vologda obl.	13.4	11.9	1.5
Murmansk obl.	11.5	6.0	5.5
North-west region	11.1	12.7	−1.6
St. Petersburg (Leningrad)	10.8	12.2	−1.4
Leningrad obl.	11.0	12.5	−1.5
Novgorod obl.	12.2	14.1	−1.9
Pskov obl.	11.9	15.1	−3.2
Central region	11.0	13.0	−2.0
Bryansk obl.	13.0	12.8	0.2
Vladimir obl.	12.1	12.5	−0.4
Ivanovo obl.	*11.6*	*14.0*	−2.4
Tver' (Kalinin) obl.	11.5	14.8	−3.3
Kaluga obl.	11.9	12.4	−0.5
Kostroma obl.	12.6	13.4	−0.8
Moscow city	10.5	12.8	−2.3
Moscow obl.	10.2	12.2	−2.0
Orel obl.	12.2	13.0	−0.8
Ryazan' obl.	11.6	14.0	−2.4
Smolensk obl.	11.8	13.2	−1.4
Tula obl.	10.2	14.4	−4.2
Yaroslavl' obl.	11.3	13.2	−1.9

	Births	Deaths	Natural increase
Volgo-Vyatka region	**13.0**	**11.9**	**1.1**
Mari ASSR	15.8	10.3	5.5
Mordvin ASSR	13.4	11.4	2.0
Chuvash ASSR	15.7	10.1	5.6
Nizhnii Novgorod (Gor'kii) obl.	11.4	13.0	−1.6
Kirov obl.	12.7	11.8	0.9
Central Black-earth region	**12.0**	**13.7**	**−1.7**
Belgorod obl.	12.9	12.8	0.1
Voronezh obl.	11.5	13.9	−2.4
Kursk obl.	11.8	13.9	−2.1
Lipetsk obl.	12.1	12.8	−0.7
Tambov obl.	11.7	14.9	−3.2
Volga region	**13.7**	**11.0**	**2.7**
Kalmyk ASSR	20.9	8.2	12.7
Tatar ASSR	15.3	9.9	5.4
Astrakhan' obl.	15.0	10.4	4.6
Volgograd obl.	13.0	11.7	1.3
Samara (Kuibyshev) obl.	12.2	11.0	1.2
Penza obl.	12.3	12.2	0.1
Saratov obl.	13.4	11.8	1.6
Ul'yanovsk obl.	14.4	11.2	2.9
North Caucasus region	**16.0**	**11.1**	**4.9**
Dagestan ASSR	26.2	6.2	20.0
Kabardino-Balkar ASSR	19.9	8.5	11.4
North Osetiya ASSR	17.1	9.6	7.5
Checheno-Ingush ASSR	24.6	8.5	16.1
Krasnodar krai	13.2	13.1	0.1
incl. Adyge AO	14.1	12.3	1.8
Stavropol krai	15.0	11.0	4.0
incl. Karachaevo-Cherkess AO	17.0	8.2	8.8
Rostov obl.	12.5	12.5	0.0

Ural' region	**14.0**	**10.4**	**3.6**
Bashkir ASSR	16.1	9.6	6.5
Udmurt ASSR	15.0	9.7	5.3
Kurgan obl.	14.5	11.4	3.1
Orenburg obl.	15.2	9.6	5.6
Perm' obl.	13.6	10.8	2.8
incl. Komi-Permyak AOk	16.6	12.1	4.5
Sverdlovsk obl.	12.2	11.2	1.0
Chelyabinsk obl.	13.3	10.5	2.8
West Siberia region	**13.9**	**9.6**	**4.3**
Altai krai	13.3	11.1	2.2
incl. Gorno-Altai AO	19.2	10.9	8.3
Kemerovo obl.	12.6	11.0	1.6
Novosibirsk obl.	12.9	10.6	2.3
Omsk obl.	14.9	9.3	5.6
Tomsk obl.	13.4	9.3	4.1
Tyumen' obl.	15.9	6.3	9.6
incl. Khanty-Mansi AOk	16.7	4.1	12.6
and Yamalo-Nenets AOk	16.3	3.3	13.0
East Siberia region	**16.1**	**9.5**	**6.6**
Buryat ASSR	18.2	9.1	9.1
Tuva ASSR	26.2	8.6	17.6
Krasnoyarsk krai	14.5	9.8	4.7
incl. Khakass AO	15.2	10.5	4.7
and Taimyr			
(Dolgano-Nenets) AOk	15.6	6.7	8.9
and Evenki AOk	20.7	7.6	13.1
Irkutsk obl.	15.8	9.8	6.0
incl. Ust'-Ordynskii			
Buryat AOk	24.5	9.6	14.9
Chita obl.	16.7	8.7	8.0
incl. Aginskii-Buryat AOk	24.1	7.8	16.3
Far East region	**15.5**	**8.2**	**7.3**
Yakut ASSR	19.6	6.8	12.8
Primor'e krai	14.7	9.1	5.6
Khabarovsk krai	15.4	9.3	6.1
incl. Jewish AO	17.8	9.5	8.3

	Births	*Deaths*	*Natural increase*
Far East region (*cont.*)			
Amur obl.	16.0	8.5	7.5
Kamchatka obl.	12.5	6.3	6.2
incl. Koryak AOk	16.1	8.7	7.4
Magadan obl.	14.0	5.2	8.8
incl. Chukot AOk	14.3	3.9	10.4
Sakhalin obl.	14.1	8.1	6.0
Kaliningrad obl.	12.6	9.8	2.8

Note: A fall in the birthrate is taking place throughout the republic. In 1990 a negative natural increase (i.e. an excess of deaths over births) was registered in 21 *oblasti*; in 1989 the corresponding figure was 10.

Source: *Nar. khoz. RSFSR 1990*, s. 99–101.

Rates* for births, deaths, natural increase and infant mortality (IMR) in cities with a population of over one million, 1990**

	Birth	Death	Natural increase	IMR
Volgograd	11.3	11.0	0.3	15.2
Ekaterinburg (Sverdlovsk)	11.7	10.0	1.7	13.5
Kazan'	13.6	10.1	3.5	18.4
Moscow	10.5	12.8	−2.3	16.8
less outlying popn. under city soviet	10.5	12.9	−2.4	16.9
Nizhnii Novgorod (Gor'kii)	10.7	11.4	−0.7	14.9
Novosibirsk	11.9	10.2	1.7	17.3
Omsk	13.5	8.7	4.8	17.8
Perm'	12.6	9.7	2.9	18.0
Rostov-na-Donu	11.2	11.9	−0.7	22.4
Samara (Kuibyshev)	11.0	11.1	−0.1	23.3
St. Petersburg (Leningrad)	10.8	12.2	−1.4	18.0
less outlying popn. under city soviet	10.8	12.3	−1.5	18.9
Ufa	13.4	8.3	5.1	21.2
Chelyabinsk	12.8	9.4	3.4	17.3

* Per thousand population. ** Deaths of infants under one year per thousand live births.

Source: *Vestnik statistiki, 1991*, 12, s. 41.

Note: The IMR data need to be adjusted upwards to be fully comparable with the figures for most developed countries. [Ed.]

Moscow 1991

The figure for the natural increase in the city of Moscow fell further to −3 per 1000 population.

Source: Article by E. Rubleva in *Moskovskaya pravda*, 1992, 18 marta, s. 18.

Russians resident in former USSR republics, at 1989 census
(thousands)

	Total population	Russians	Col. 2 as % of col. 1
Ukrainian SSR	51 707	11 356	22.0
Belorussian SSR	10 200	1 342	13.2
Uzbek SSR	19 905	1 653	8.3
Kazakh SSR	16 536	6 228	37.7
Georgian SSR	5 443	341	6.3
Azerbaidzhanian SSR	7 038	392	5.6
Lithuanian SSR	3 690	344	9.3
Moldavian SSR	4 338	562	13.0
Latvian SSR	2 680	906	33.8
Kirgiz SSR	4 290	917	21.4
Tadzhik SSR	5 109	388	6.0
Armenian SSR	3 288	52	1.6
Turkmen SSR	3 534	334	9.5
Estonian SSR	1 573	475	30.2

Sources of cols. 1 and 2:   *Nar. khoz. SSSR 1989*, s. 17; *Literaturnaya gazeta, 1991*, 40, s. 2.

Russians resident in former USSR republics who spoke the language of the republic, at 1989 census (thousands)

	Total	Speaking language of republic*	Col. 2 as % of col. 1
Ukrainian SSR	11 356	3 722	32.8
Belorussian SSR	1 342	329	24.5
Uzbek SSR	1 653	75	4.5
Kazakh SSR	6 228	53	0.9
Georgian SSR	341	77	22.6
Azerbaidzhanian SSR	392	56	14.3
Lithuanian SSR	344	115	33.4
Moldavian SSR	562	63	11.2
Latvian SSR	906	191	21.1
Kirgiz SSR	917	11	1.2
Tadzhik SSR	388	13	3.4
Armenian SSR	52	17	32.9
Turkmen SSR	334	8	2.4
Estonian SSR	475	65	13.7

* As reported by respondents themselves.
Source of cols. 1 and 2: *Literaturnaya gazeta*, 1991, 40, s. 2.

Refugees, 1992

The demographic situation is significantly affected by the problem of persons who are forced to leave their place of permanent residence due to the exacerbation of inter-ethnic conflicts. According to data supplied by the Russian Ministry of Internal Affairs, the number of refugees stood at 320 000 on 1 July 1992. Of that total, one-third have arrived within the last six months. A very tense situation has arisen in the North Caucasus region, which accounts for over 240 000 refugees. The mounting numbers in overpopulated regions is creating additional sources of social tension, problems of accommodation and daily life, and difficulties in finding work.

Source: *Ekonomika i zhizn'*, 1992, 30, s. 5.

Emigration, 1980–90

Year	Numbers*
1980	6 960
1985	2 943
1987	9 697
1988	20 705
1989	47 521
1990	103 609

* Persons who had received official permission to leave the former USSR for permanent residence abroad.

Note: In 1990, as in the previous year, approximately 40 per cent of emigrants from the RSFSR were inhabitants of St. Petersburg, Leningrad region, the city of Moscow, Orenburg and Omsk regions and the Kabardino-Balkar ASSR.

Source: *Nar. khoz. SSSR 1990*, s. 95–6.

5 Marriages, Divorces and Families

Marriages, 1979–90

Years	Thousands	Per 1000 population
1979	1535.5	11.1
1980	1464.6	10.6
1981	1472.8	10.6
1982	1460.2	10.4
1983	1479.1	10.5
1984	1367.8	9.6
1985	1389.4	9.7
1986	1417.5	9.8
1987	1442.6	9.9
1988	1397.4	9.5
1989	1384.3	9.4
1990	1320	8.9

Sources: *Demograficheskii ezhegodnik SSSR 1990*, s. 220; *Vestnik statistiki, 1991*, 7, s. 19.

Inter-ethnic marriages

Within the RSFSR the proportions of Russian men who married women of a different nationality were 9.7 and 9.8 per cent in, respectively, 1988 and 1989. The proportion of Russian women who married men of another nationality was 11.1 per cent in both years.

Sources: *Nar. khoz. SSSR 1989*, s. 35; *Nar. khoz. SSSR 1990*, s. 84.

Russians who marry a person of another nationality as a percentage of all Russians marrying outside Russia in republics of the former USSR, 1989

Republic	Russian men	Russian women
Ukrainian SSR	57.4	57.7
Belorussian SSR	74.6	74.5
Uzbek SSR	24.2	30.9
Kazakh SSR	24.5	27.2
Georgian SSR	42.9	55.9
Azerbaidzhanian SSR	27.2	46.3
Lithuanian SSR	58.2	54.1
Moldavian SSR	61.7	59.7
Latvian SSR	37.3	37.7
Kirgiz SSR	18.8	22.4
Tadzhik SSR	25.0	32.3
Armenian SSR	43.7	65.8
Turkmen SSR	26.2	34.9
Estonian SSR	24.3	27.3

Source: Nar. khoz. SSSR 1990, s. 84–5.

Married persons per 1000 persons of specified sex and age group, at 1989 census

Ages	Men	Women
16–17	11	37
18–19	48	230
20–24	381	618
25–29	742	798
30–39	830	813
40–49	846	754
50–59	870	674
60 and over	831	332

Source: *Vozrast naseleniya SSSR*, s. 107.

Married persons per 1000 urban and rural population of specified sex and age group, at 1989 census

Ages	Urban		Rural	
	Men	*Women*	*Men*	*Women*
16–17	11	31	9	62
18–19	50	201	42	361
20–24	383	589	376	713
25–29	743	779	735	858
30–39	833	798	820	871
40–49	846	737	846	816
50–59	863	658	887	712
60 and over	824	331	847	333

Source: *Vozrast naseleniya SSSR*, s. 108–9.

Marital status of population aged 16 and over per 1000 population of specified sex and age group, at 1989 census

Key to columns: 1 Married
                 2 Never married
                 3 Widowers/widows
                 4 Divorced and separated

Ages	1	2	3	4
Men				
Total	718	196	25	57
16–19	29	964	0	1
20–24	381	595	0	15
25–29	742	208	1	44
30–34	821	105	2	69
35–39	840	68	4	86
40–44	845	47	8	97
45–49	847	37	17	97
50–54	863	26	25	83
55–59	880	17	41	60
60–64	878	12	65	42
65–69	863	11	93	29
70 and over	748	9	223	16
Women				
Total	598	132	182	85
16–19	130	859	1	4
20–24	618	335	3	38
25–29	798	120	7	71
30–34	822	69	13	94
35–39	804	53	25	116
40–44	772	45	43	138
45–49	737	35	85	141
50–54	708	33	128	129
55–59	636	42	214	105
60–64	532	57	318	90
65–69	399	71	455	71
70 and over	162	47	752	34

Source: Nar. khoz. RSFSR 1989, s. 93.

Marital status of men aged 16 and over per 1000 male population of corresponding ages: by economic regions and major territorial-administrative divisions, at 1989 census

Key to columns:
1 Married
2 Never married
3 Widowers
4 Divorced and separated

	1	2	3	4
Russian SFSR	**718**	**196**	**25**	**57**
Northern region	**689**	**228**	**20**	**60**
Karelian ASSR	703	218	22	56
Komi ASSR	661	251	18	68
Arkhangel'sk obl.	678	238	22	60
incl. Nenets AOk	647	276	16	58
Vologda obl.	709	214	24	51
Murmansk obl.	703	215	14	63
North-west region	**698**	**199**	**28**	**67**
St. Petersburg (Leningrad)*	679	218	26	68
Leningrad obl.	730	169	27	67
Novgorod obl.	730	170	30	65
Pskov obl.	724	174	33	64
Central region	**721**	**182**	**29**	**64**
Bryansk obl.	734	186	27	51
Vladimir obl.	740	174	27	58
Ivanovo obl.	730	176	30	62
Tver' (Kalinin) obl.	731	172	31	63
Kaluga obl.	721	190	26	62
Kostroma obl.	733	188	28	50
Moscow*	715	184	29	68
Moscow obl.	718	180	28	67
Orel obl.	724	188	29	55
Ryazan' obl.	721	194	29	55
Smolensk obl.	721	183	29	65
Tula obl.	725	171	33	70
Yaroslavl' obl.	714	189	28	67

	1	*2*	*3*	*4*
Volgo-Vyatka region	727	199	26	45
Mari ASSR	710	226	25	35
Mordvin ASSR	719	211	26	42
Chuvash ASSR	701	236	27	32
Nizhnii Novgorod				
(Gor'kii) obl.	739	181	27	50
Kirov obl.	731	196	23	49
Central Black-earth region	735	180	30	52
Belgorod obl.	760	162	28	43
Voronezh obl.	733	180	31	54
Kursk obl.	737	180	31	48
Lipetsk obl.	722	188	29	59
Tambov obl.	722	191	32	53
Volga region	723	195	25	54
Kalmyk ASSR	685	242	28	42
Tatar ASSR	719	216	21	41
Astrakhan' obl.	711	203	25	57
Volgograd obl.	724	181	28	65
Samara (Kuibyshev) obl.	726	188	25	58
Penza obl.	735	187	26	50
Saratov obl.	718	190	26	60
Ul'yanovsk obl.	740	192	22	45
North Caucasus region	721	194	27	51
Dagestan ASSR	688	239	19	21
Kabardino-Balkar ASSR	708	229	23	36
North Osetiya ASSR	647	282	25	42
Checheno-Ingush ASSR	642	296	23	34
Krasnodar krai	739	170	29	60
incl. Adyge AO	733	180	27	58
Stavropol' krai	733	184	26	55
incl. Karachaevo-				
Cherkess AO	704	229	23	42
Rostov obl.	739	168	29	58

Ural' region	**722**	**202**	**23**	**50**
Bashkir ASSR	721	219	20	37
Udmurt ASSR	724	212	22	40
Kurgan obl.	744	181	22	50
Orenburg obl.	737	193	22	45
Perm' obl.	701	216	24	54
incl. Komi-Permyak AOk	707	223	28	36
Sverdlovsk obl.	722	191	25	59
Chelyabinsk obl.	726	192	24	56
West Siberia region	**734**	**187**	**21**	**55**
Altai krai	754	170	22	52
incl. Gorno-Altai AO	735	186	26	51
Kemerovo obl.	733	175	26	64
Novosibirsk obl.	733	186	22	57
Omsk obl.	727	198	21	52
Tomsk obl.	695	224	21	58
Tyumen' obl.	735	194	14	49
incl. Khanty-Mansi AOk	750	183	9	52
and Yamalo-Nenets AOk	758	183	7	46
East Siberia region	**707**	**207**	**24**	**58**
Buryat ASSR	702	224	26	46
Tuva ASSR	656	271	35	34
Krasnoyarsk krai	713	196	22	65
incl. Khakass AO	724	178	25	70
and Taimyr (Dolgano-Nenets) AOk	668	245	17	67
and Evenki AOk	681	223	21	71
Irkutsk obl.	701	206	26	62
incl. Ust'-Ordynskii Buryat AOk	679	245	29	39
Chita obl.	714	217	24	43
incl. Aginskii-Buryat AOk	654	280	25	39
Far East region	**689**	**224**	**20**	**63**
Yakut ASSR	683	239	22	53
Primor'e krai	686	225	22	64
Khabarovsk krai	682	220	22	69
incl. Jewish AO	741	170	22	59

	1	2	3	4
Far East region (*cont.*)				
Amur obl.	707	217	20	52
Kamchatka obl.	656	258	14	70
incl. Koryak AOk	677	214	23	83
Magadan obl.	719	193	11	73
incl. Chukot AOk	760	171	9	57
Sakhalin obl.	687	224	20	66
Kaliningrad obl.	695	219	22	62

* The figure includes outlying settlements which are administratively subordinate to the city.

Source: *Sotsial'noe razvitie RSFSR 1990, Tom II*, s. 152–7.

Marital status of women aged 16 and over per 1000 female population of corresponding ages: by economic regions and major territorial-administrative divisions, at 1989 census

Key to columns: 1 Married
2 Never married
3 Widowers
4 Divorced and separated

	1	2	3	4
Russian SFSR	598	132	182	85
Northern region	622	134	161	81
Karelian ASSR	610	139	172	78
Komi ASSR	651	137	131	80
Arkhangel'sk obl.	613	137	175	74
incl. Nenets AOk	644	160	135	60
Vologda obl.	590	143	201	64
Murmansk obl.	657	112	113	114
North-west region	549	148	191	106
St. Petersburg (Leningrad)*	527	167	179	120
Leningrad obl.	594	114	190	96
Novgorod obl.	575	124	223	74
Pskov obl.	575	119	235	66
Central region	566	136	198	97
Bryansk obl.	584	128	212	74
Vladimir obl.	584	137	198	80
Ivanovo obl.	560	144	212	82
Tver' (Kalinin) obl.	563	125	234	75
Kaluga obl.	584	128	202	85
Kostroma obl.	587	137	210	65
Moscow*	549	147	180	121
Moscow obl.	571	136	183	104
Orel obl.	580	125	218	73
Ryazan' obl.	575	127	228	69
Smolensk obl.	576	125	218	80
Tula obl.	575	110	220	94
Yaroslavl' obl.	563	140	210	86

	1	2	3	4
Volgo-Vyatka region	**583**	**143**	**206**	**65**
Mari ASSR	585	158	193	58
Mordvin ASSR	569	154	219	56
Chuvash ASSR	567	179	195	54
Nizhnii Novgorod (Gor'kii) obl.	583	130	209	75
Kirov obl.	602	132	208	57
Central Black-earth region	**584**	**123**	**221**	**69**
Belgorod obl.	596	124	207	64
Voronezh obl.	581	124	218	75
Kursk obl.	588	120	227	61
Lipetsk obl.	581	127	216	75
Tambov obl.	575	121	239	63
Volga region	**599**	**130**	**189**	**79**
Kalmyk ASSR	630	164	147	57
Tatar ASSR	590	151	188	67
Astrakhan' obl.	610	119	185	83
Volgograd obl.	600	115	188	95
Samara (Kuibyshev) obl.	599	128	180	90
Penza obl.	592	128	211	67
Saratov obl.	598	119	193	84
Ul'yanovsk obl.	610	134	191	64
North Caucasus region	**596**	**123**	**187**	**87**
Dagestan ASSR	586	167	148	58
Kabardino-Balkar ASSR	590	153	172	81
North Osetiya ASSR	530	190	192	84
Checheno-Ingush ASSR	540	200	171	83
Krasnodar krai	603	100	202	93
incl. Adyge AO	592	113	202	91
Stavropol' krai	607	114	186	91
incl. Karachaevo- Cherkess AO	590	147	174	87
Rostov obl.	609	108	188	90

Ural' region	**606**	**135**	**179**	**77**
Bashkir ASSR	609	141	183	64
Udmurt ASSR	595	161	179	63
Kurgan obl.	615	122	187	73
Orenburg obl.	626	120	178	73
Perm' obl.	595	146	178	76
incl. Komi-Permyak AOk	592	151	210	41
Sverdlovsk obl.	600	133	178	87
Chelyabinsk obl.	610	125	174	89
West Siberia region	**640**	**121**	**155**	**81**
Altai krai	637	112	173	76
incl. Gorno-Altai AO	632	153	154	59
Kemerovo obl.	637	105	168	88
Novosibirsk obl.	610	128	169	91
Omsk obl.	614	139	162	83
Tomsk obl.	635	144	144	75
Tyumen' obl.	700	121	106	68
incl. Khanty-Mansi AOk	761	102	61	72
and Yamalo-Nenets AOk	781	105	43	67
East Siberia region	**644**	**128**	**147**	**78**
Buryat ASSR	636	151	148	63
Tuva ASSR	618	207	124	48
Krasnoyarsk krai	647	119	149	82
incl. Khakass AO	651	110	159	77
and Taimyr				
(Dolgano-Nenets) AOk	681	135	82	99
and Evenki AOk	737	118	87	57
Irkutsk obl.	633	128	150	84
incl. Ust'-Ordynskii				
Buryat AOk	642	145	167	38
Chita obl.	671	120	140	67
incl. Aginskii-Buryat AOk	636	171	141	50
Far East region	**667**	**124**	**119**	**87**
Yakut ASSR	666	120	152	104
Primor'e krai	652	165	99	67
Khabarovsk krai	650	126	131	87
incl. Jewish AO	680	114	132	69

	1	2	3	4
Far East region (*cont.*)				
Amur obl.	690	110	129	68
Kamchatka obl.	698	113	82	106
incl. Koryak AOk	706	125	86	81
Magadan obl.	730	103	62	104
incl. Chukot AOk	771	97	43	87
Sakhalin obl.	667	114	118	99
Kaliningrad obl.	622	120	152	104

* The figure includes outlying settlements which are administratively subordinate to the city.

Source: *Sotsial'noe razvitie RSFSR 1990, Tom II*, s. 158–63.

Marriages and divorces per 1000 population in cities with a population of over one million, 1990

	Marriages	*Divorces*
Volgograd	9.5	5.2
Ekaterinburg (Sverdlovsk)	9.4	3.9
Kazan'	8.9	3.7
Moscow	9.4	4.8
less outlying popn. under city soviet	9.4	4.8
Nizhnii Novgorod (Gor'kii)	8.6	3.4
Novosibirsk	9.8	4.9
Omsk	10.3	5.4
Perm'	8.5	3.5
Rostov-na-Donu	10.2	5.4
Samara (Kuibyshev)	8.9	4.3
St. Petersburg (Leningrad)	10.3	5.5
less outlying popn. under city soviet	10.4	5.6
Ufa	7.6	2.3
Chelyabinsk	9.1	4.3

Source: *Vestnik statistiki, 1991*, 12, s. 41.

Divorces, 1958–90

Years	Thousands	Per 1000 population	Per 1000 married couples
1958–59	—	—	6.5
1960	—	1.5	—
1969–70	—	—	13.3
1970	—	3.0	—
1978–79	—	—	17.5
1979	593.9	4.3	—
1980	580.7	4.2	—
1981	577.5	4.1	—
1982	557.6	4.0	—
1983	583.0	4.1	—
1984	573.7	4.0	—
1984–85	—	—	16.2
1985	574.0	4.0	—
1986	579.4	4.0	—
1987	580.1	4.0	—
1988	573.9	3.9	—
1989	582.5	3.9	—
1990	560.0	3.8	—

Note: The low birth rate in Russia is associated with the high rate of divorce among married couples. Although the number of divorces in recent years has not exceeded the peak figure in 1983 it should be noted that the number of marriages has declined, a trend which is linked to the smaller contingent of infants born at the end of the 1960s and early 1970s.

A third of all the marriages which end in divorce are of young couples whose union has lasted for less than 5 years. Throughout a lifetime more than half of all married men and women end their union. At the 1979 census 39 men per 1000 male population were divorced and the rate had risen to 56 per 1000 at the 1989 census. The corresponding figures for women were 74 and 85 per 1000.

Sources: *Naselenie SSSR 1987*, s. 208; *Demograficheskii ezhegodnik SSSR 1990*, s. 220; *Vestnik statistiki*, 1991, 7, s. 19, 21.

The procedure for obtaining a divorce was substantially simplified in 1965. [Ed.]

Number of divorces by age of divorcees, 1989

Age	Men	Women
Under 18	22	329
18–19	1 276	9 274
20–24	58 974	100 861
25–29	139 527	135 908
30–34	122 667	112 095
35–39	90 784	81 936
40–44	56 306	48 944
45–49	34 606	29 404
50–54	34 729	29 736
55–59	16 480	13 833
60 and over	18 856	14 353
age unknown	8 273	5 827
Total divorces	**582 500**	**582 500**

Source: *Demograficheskii ezhegodnik SSSR 1990*, s. 302–3.

Divorces by number of children per divorcing couples, 1989

Number of children under age 18	Number of divorces
0	223 585
1	253 146
2	94 362
3 and more	11 407
Total divorces	**582 500**

Note: There were 822.4 children per 1000 divorces in 1989.
Source: *Demograficheskii ezhegodnik SSSR 1990*, s. 304.

Divorces by duration of marriage, 1989

Number of years	Number of divorces
Under 1	23 156
1	46 018
2	51 481
3	47 342
4	41 749
5–9	155 025
10–14	91 319
15–19	17 632
20 and over	70 343
Duration unknown	387
Total divorces	**582 500**

Source: *Demograficheskii ezhegodnik SSSR 1990*, s. 306–7.

Number and size distribution of families,*
at censuses of 1979 and 1989

| | Thousands | | Percentages | |
	1979	1989	1979	1989
Total population				
All families	36 725	40 246	100	100
With:				
2	11 608	13 759	31.6	34.2
3	11 589	11 281	31.5	28.0
4	8 588	10 154	23.4	25.2
5	3 149	3 354	8.6	8.3
6	1 093	1 106	3.0	2.8
7 and more members	698	592	1.9	1.5
Urban population				
All families	25 560	29 663	100	100
With:				
2	7 788	9 824	30.5	33.1
3	8 655	8 788	33.9	29.6
4	6 274	7 736	24.6	26.1
5	2 004	2 311	7.8	7.8
6	573	698	2.2	2.3
7 and more members	266	306	1.0	1.1
Rural population				
All families	11 165	10 583	100	100
With:				
2	3 820	3 935	34.2	37.2
3	2 934	2 493	26.3	23.6
4	2 314	2 418	20.7	22.8
5	1 145	1 043	10.3	9.9
6	520	408	4.6	3.9
7 and more members	432	286	3.9	2.6

* According to the census definition, the term 'family' denotes a group of persons who are permanently resident together, are directly connected by kinship or marriage and share a common budget.

Source: *Nar. khoz. RSFSR 1989*, s. 95, 652.

Members of families and single persons, at censuses of 1979 and 1989

| | *Thousands* | | *Percentages* | |
	1979	*1989*	*1979*	*1989*
	Total population			
Total	137 410	147 022	100	100
Family members				
living with family	120 057	129 971	87.4	88.4
living separately	7 772	6 925	5.6	4.7
Single persons	9 581	10 126	7.0	6.9
	Urban population			
Total	94 942	107 959	100	100
Family members				
living with family	82 135	95 051	86.5	88.0
living separately	6 237	5 567	6.6	5.2
Single persons	6 570	7 341	6.9	6.8
	Rural population			
Total	42 468	39 063	100	100
Family members				
living with family	37 922	34 920	89.3	89.4
living separately	1 535	1 358	3.6	3.5
Single persons	3 011	2 785	7.1	7.1

Source: *Nar. khoz. RSFSR 1989*, s. 94.

**Size distribution of families in towns and urban-type
settlements, at censuses of 1979 and 1989** (percentages)

	1979	1989
Total urban population		
All families	100	100
With:		
2	30.5	33.1
3	33.9	29.6
4	24.6	26.1
5	7.8	7.8
6	2.2	2.3
7	0.6	0.7
8	0.2	0.2
9	0.1	0.1
10 and more members	0.1	0.1
Residents in towns		
All families	100*	100*
With:		
2	30.3	33.0
3	34.0	29.9
4	24.6	25.9
5	7.9	7.8
6	2.2	2.4
7	0.6	0.6
8	0.2	0.2
9	0.1	0.1
10 and more members	0.1	0.1
Residents in urban-type settlements		
All families	100**	100**
With:		
2	31.6	33.8
3	32.9	27.9
4	24.3	27.1
5	7.7	7.9

6	2.3	2.2
7	0.7	0.7
8	0.3	0.2
9	0.1	0.1
10 and more members	0.1	0.1

* Number of families: 22 236 549 in 1979 and 25 894 012 in 1989.
** Number of families: 3 323 222 in 1979 and 3 769 331 in 1989.

Source: *Gorodskie poseleniya*, s. 60–1.

Average number of persons per family,* at censuses of 1979 and 1989

	1979	1989
Total population	3.3	3.2
Urban population	3.2	3.2
Rural population	3.4	3.3

* Excluding family members who live separately.

Source: *Nar. khoz. RSFSR 1989*, s. 94.

Percentage distribution of families by number of children under 16 years, 1989

	1	2	3	4	5 and more
Families of blue- and white-collar workers*	54.2	38.3	6.0	1.1	0.4
Families of collective farmers*	40.1	39.6	14.5	3.9	1.9

* From a random sample of 310 000 families interviewed in March 1989.

Source: *Sotsial'noe razvitie SSSR*, s. 286–7.

Single-parent families, at censuses of 1979 and 1989 (thousands)

	1979	1989
Total		
Mothers with children	4358	4890
Fathers with children	301	403
Mothers with children and one parent*	690	739
Fathers with children and one parent*	62	77
Urban families		
Mothers with children	3128	3857
Fathers with children	218	312
Mothers with children and one parent*	511	621
Fathers with children and one parent*	43	58
Rural families		
Mothers with children	1 230	1 033
Fathers with children	83	91
Mothers with children and one parent*	179	118
Fathers with children and one parent*	19	19

* Of the mother or the father.

Source: *Nar. khoz. RSFSR 1990*, s. 96.

6 Sex and Age Structure

Sex composition of the population, 1959–1991

Year	Thousands		Percentages	
	Men	Women	Men	Women
1959	52.4	65.1	45	55
1970	59.3	70.8	46	54
1979	63.5	74.1	46	54
1989	69.0	78.4	47	53
1990	69.4	78.6	47	53
1991	69.7	78.8	47	53

Source: *Nar. khoz. RSFSR 1990*, s. 76.

Number of women per 1000 men, at censuses of 1979 and 1989

Year	Total	Urban	Rural
	Population present at census		
1979	1167	1163	1176
1989	1135	1142	1117
	*Permanent population**		
1979	1174	1170	1183
1989	1140	1145	1125

* Includes persons temporarily absent at time of censuses.
Source: *Kratkaya kharakteristika naseleniya RSFSR: Chast' I*, s. 34.

Distribution of population by age group and sex ratio, 1991

	Thousands	Percentage	Women per 1000 men
All ages	**148 164**	**100**	**1 134**
Under 5	11 300	7.6	958
5–9	11 779	8.0	967
10–14	10 815	7.3	971
15–19	10 237	6.9	971
20–24	9 492	6.4	948
25–29	11 387	7.7	968
30–34	12 996	8.8	986
35–39	12 156	8.2	1 006
40–44	10 232	6.9	1 030
45–49	5 667	3.8	1 094
50–54	10 518	7.1	1 160
55–59	7 593	5.1	1 240
60–64	8 893	6.0	1 424
65–69	5 580	3.8	2 214
70 and over	9 519	6.4	3 214
Under working age	35 993	24.3	966
Of working age*	83 976	56.7	935
Over working age	28 195	19.0	2 656

* Men: 16–59 years; women: 16–54 years.

Source: *Nar. khoz. RSFSR 1990*, s. 86.

Distribution of urban population by age group and sex ratio, 1991

	Thousands	*Percentage*	*Women per 1000 men*
All ages	**109 332**	**100**	**1 139**
Under 5	7 972	7.3	956
5–9	8 416	7.7	964
10–14	7 789	7.1	970
15–19	7 848	7.2	1 013
20–24	7 342	6.7	940
25–29	8 545	7.8	995
30–34	9 861	9.0	1 024
35–39	9 462	8.7	1 043
40–44	8 167	7.5	1 061
45–49	4 393	4.0	1 105
50–54	7 788	7.1	1 178
55–59	5 310	4.9	1 276
60–64	6 156	5.6	1 427
65–69	3 902	3.6	2 208
70 and over	6 381	5.8	2 969
Under working age	25 704	23.5	964
Of working age*	64 212	58.7	966
Over working age	19 416	17.8	2 622

* Men: 16–59 years; women: 16–54 years.

Source: *Nar. khoz. RSFSR 1990*, s. 87.

Distribution of rural population by age group and sex ratio, 1991

	Thousands	*Percentage*	*Women per 1000 men*
All ages	**38 832**	**100**	**1 120**
Under 5	3 328	8.6	962
5–9	3 363	8.7	975
10–14	3 026	7.8	974
15–19	2 389	6.2	845
20–24	2 150	5.5	978
25–29	2 842	7.3	889
30–34	3 135	8.1	875
35–39	2 694	6.9	886
40–44	2 065	5.3	918
45–49	1 274	3.3	1 057
50–54	2 730	7.0	1 108
55–59	2 283	5.9	1 159
60–64	2 737	7.0	1 420
65–69	1 678	4.3	2 230
70 and over	3 138	8.1	3 480
Under working age	10 289	26.5	969
Of working age*	19 764	50.9	840
Over working age	8 779	22.6	2 734

* Men: 16–59 years; women: 16–54 years.

Source: *Nar. khoz. RSFSR 1990*, s. 88.

The shortage of brides in rural areas

In rural areas a substantial disproportion in the sex and age structure of the population has created real difficulties for men seeking marriage partners. In 1989 for every 1000 men in rural areas in the age group 20–39 there were only 886 women of that age. (In 1979 the corresponding figure stood at 911 and in 1970 at 973.)

In Arkhangel'sk *oblast'* for every 1000 men in this age group there were 789 women; in Volgograd *oblast'* and Mordoviya the figure was 774; in Ryazan', Pskov and Kursk *oblasti* the figures were 785, 789 and 790 respectively, while in both Tambov and Orel *oblasti* the figure was 798.

In those and in a further 39 territorial-administrative areas the proportion of women in ages when high marriage rates obtain has been falling throughout the last twenty-year period.

The problem of 'the shortage of brides' is becoming more serious due to the substantial migration of young women to the towns. As a result, in Russia as a whole, for every 1000 unmarried men aged 20–39 in the countryside there are half as many unmarried women. In the areas specified above the figure declines towards one-third.

Source: *Vestnik statistiki*, 1991, 7, s. 21.

The effect of rural depopulation

Over several decades the high levels of migration of young people to the towns has created a deformation in the age, sex and marital structures of the rural population. For example, in all the *oblasti* of the Central and Central Black-earth regions, persons of pension age constitute 30–35 per cent of those who live in the countryside, but the corresponding figure for women of child-bearing age (15–49 years) is only 16–17 per cent.

Source: *Vestnik statistiki*, 1991, 7, s. 24.

Percentage of population of economic regions and major territorial-administrative divisions in working and non-working age groups*, at 1989 census

	Below	Of working age	Over
Russian SFSR	**24.5**	**56.9**	**18.5**
urban	**23.8**	**58.9**	**17.2**
rural	**26.4**	**51.5**	**22.1**
Northern region	**26.4**	**59.4**	**14.2**
urban	**26.4**	**61.1**	**12.4**
rural	**26.7**	**53.5**	**19.8**
Karelian ASSR	25.6	58.4	16.0
Komi ASSR	27.9	62.1	10.0
Arkhangel'sk obl.	26.6	58.0	15.4
incl. Nenets AOk	30.9	61.4	7.7
Vologda obl.	24.5	55.1	20.4
Murmansk obl.	27.3	63.9	8.6
North-west region	**20.9**	**57.9**	**21.0**
urban	**20.8**	**59.0**	**20.0**
rural	**21.6**	**50.7**	**27.5**
St. Petersburg (Leningrad)**	19.8	59.5	20.5
Leningrad obl.	23.4	56.3	20.0
Novgorod obl.	22.3	54.9	22.8
Pskov obl.	21.0	54.2	24.8
Central region	**20.8**	**56.8**	**22.3**
urban	**21.0**	**58.1**	**20.7**
rural	**20.6**	**49.9**	**29.3**
Bryansk obl.	22.9	53.8	23.3
Vladimir obl.	22.3	56.4	21.3
Ivanovo obl.	21.1	55.3	23.6
Tver' (Kalinin) obl.	20.9	54.0	25.1
Kaluga obl.	22.2	56.6	21.2
Kostroma obl.	22.6	54.7	22.7

Moscow**	19.8	58.5	21.7
Moscow obl.	21.0	57.8	20.6
Orel obl.	21.1	55.9	23.0
Ryazan' obl.	20.3	55.6	24.1
Smolensk obl.	22.3	54.7	23.0
Tula obl.	19.8	55.2	25.0
Yaroslavl' obl.	21.4	56.2	22.4
Volgo-Vyatka region	**23.6**	**55.7**	**20.7**
urban	**23.6**	**58.6**	**17.8**
rural	**23.8**	**49.2**	**27.0**
Mari ASSR	27.1	55.8	17.1
Mordvin ASSR	23.6	55.7	20.7
Chuvash ASSR	26.9	55.5	17.6
Nizhnii Novgorod (Gor'kii) obl.	21.6	55.9	22.5
Kirov obl.	24.1	55.2	20.7
Central Black-earth region	**21.5**	**54.5**	**24.0**
urban	**23.0**	**58.7**	**18.3**
rural	**19.1**	**48.3**	**32.6**
Belgorod obl.	22.8	54.1	23.1
Voronezh obl.	20.7	54.5	24.8
Kursk obl.	21.6	54.0	24.4
Lipetsk obl.	21.5	56.1	22.4
Tambov obl.	21.1	54.1	24.8
Volga region	**24.2**	**57.0**	**18.8**
urban	**23.8**	**59.0**	**17.2**
rural	**25.0**	**51.6**	**23.4**
Kalmyk ASSR	32.2	56.9	10.9
Tatar ASSR	25.4	56.8	17.8
Astrakhan' obl.	26.1	56.6	17.3
Volgograd obl.	23.3	56.4	20.3
Samara (Kuibyshev) obl.	23.6	58.0	18.4
Penza obl.	22.5	55.9	21.6
Saratov obl.	23.3	57.4	19.3
Ul'yanovsk obl.	24.0	57.0	19.0

	Below	Of working age	Over
North Caucasus region	**26.4**	**55.0**	**18.6**
urban	**24.5**	**57.0**	**18.5**
rural	**29.0**	**52.2**	**18.8**
Dagestan ASSR	36.3	51.7	12.0
Kabardino-Balkar ASSR	29.6	55.9	14.5
North Osetiya ASSR	26.7	55.4	17.9
Checheno-Ingush ASSR	33.8	52.8	13.4
Krasnodar krai	23.7	54.6	21.6
incl. Adyge AO	24.7	54.2	21.1
Stavropol krai	25.9	55.3	18.8
incl. Karachaevo-Cherkess AO	28.9	55.1	16.0
Rostov obl.	22.9	56.8	20.3
Ural' region	**25.7**	**56.5**	**17.7**
urban	**24.7**	**58.2**	**17.0**
rural	**28.6**	**51.3**	**20.1**
Bashkir ASSR	26.7	56.0	17.3
Udmurt ASSR	27.3	56.7	16.0
Kurgan obl.	25.8	55.2	19.0
Orenburg obl.	26.6	56.1	17.3
Perm' obl.	25.5	56.6	17.4
incl. Komi-Permyak AOk	29.1	50.7	19.6
Sverdlovsk obl.	24.6	57.0	18.4
Chelyabinsk obl.	25.0	56.8	18.2
West Siberia region	**27.0**	**57.6**	**15.4**
urban	**26.0**	**59.6**	**14.4**
rural	**29.8**	**52.3**	**17.9**
Altai krai	26.4	55.5	18.1
incl. Gorno-Altai AO	32.5	52.9	14.6
Kemerovo obl.	25.4	57.1	17.5
Novosibirsk obl.	24.9	57.3	17.8
Omsk obl.	27.6	56.4	16.0
Tomsk obl.	27.1	58.7	14.2
Tyumen' obl.	30.7	61.0	8.3
incl. Khanty-Mansi AOk	33.2	63.3	3.5
and Yamalo-Nenets AOk	32.8	65.2	2.0

East Siberia region	**29.1**	**57.7**	**13.2**
urban	27.6	59.7	12.7
rural	32.6	52.7	14.7
Buryat ASSR	31.7	55.8	12.5
Tuva ASSR	37.3	54.9	7.8
Krasnoyarsk krai	27.2	58.8	14.0
incl. Khakass AO	28.3	56.5	15.2
and Taimyr			
(Dolgano-Nenets) AOk	30.9	64.8	4.3
and Evenki AOk	32.7	62.4	4.9
Irkutsk obl.	28.3	58.2	13.5
incl. Ust'-Ordynskii			
Buryat AOk	35.1	51.0	13.9
Chita obl.	30.9	56.5	12.6
incl. Aginskii-Buryat AOk	38.7	51.0	10.3
Far East region	**28.1**	**61.5**	**10.4**
urban	26.8	62.7	10.5
rural	32.3	57.6	10.1
Yakut ASSR	32.5	61.0	6.5
Primor'e krai	26.2	60.9	12.9
Khabarovsk krai	27.3	60.4	12.3
incl. Jewish AO	30.9	56.4	12.7
Amur obl.	29.0	59.1	11.9
Kamchatka obl.	28.2	66.5	5.3
incl. Koryak AOk	31.4	63.5	5.1
Magadan obl.	29.4	66.9	3.7
incl. Chukot AOk	30.6	67.5	1.9
Sakhalin obl.	27.2	62.7	10.1
Kaliningrad obl.	23.5	59.7	16.8

* The working age for men was 16–59 and for women 16–54 years.
** The figure includes outlying settlements which are administratively subordinate to the city.

Source: *Vozrast naseleniya*, s. 24–41.

7 Women in Society

Sex ratios in economic regions and major territorial-administrative divisions, at 1989 census

	Women as % of population	Men per 1000 women
Russian SFSR	**53.3**	**877**
urban	**53.4**	**873**
rural	**52.9**	**889**
Northern region	**51.3**	**950**
urban	**51.4**	**945**
rural	**50.8**	**967**
Karelian ASSR	52.4	908
urban	52.6	903
rural	51.8	930
Komi ASSR	49.4	1023
urban	49.7	1012
rural	48.6	1058
Arkhangel'sk obl.	51.3	948
urban	51.6	938
rural	50.6	977
incl. Nenets AOk	48.2	1073
urban	47.5	1104
rural	49.5	1021
Vologda obl.	53.3	878
urban	53.5	869
rural	52.8	894
Murmansk obl.	50.2	992
urban	50.4	984
rural	47.9	1089

North-west region	**54.6**	**830**
urban	**54.7**	**829**
rural	**54.4**	**838**
St. Petersburg		
(Leningrad)*	55.0	819
Leningrad obl.	53.9	856
urban	54.0	854
rural	53.7	861
Novgorod obl.	54.4	840
urban	53.9	855
rural	55.3	807
Pskov obl.	54.3	841
urban	54.0	853
rural	54.9	821
Central region	**54.7**	**829**
urban	**54.6**	**830**
rural	**55.0**	**820**
Bryansk obl.	54.3	841
urban	53.6	864
rural	55.7	795
Vladimir obl.	54.6	833
urban	54.3	841
rural	55.4	804
Ivanovo obl.	55.2	812
urban	55.4	804
rural	54.0	850
Tver' (Kalinin) obl.	55.0	820
urban	54.6	832
rural	55.9	790
Kaluga obl.	53.9	854
urban	53.6	866
rural	54.7	827
Kostroma obl.	54.1	847
urban	54.2	845
rural	54.0	853
Moscow*	55.1	814
urban	55.1	814
rural	60.0	667

	Women as % of population	Men per 1000 women
Central region (*cont.*)		
Moscow obl.	54.5	835
urban	54.5	835
rural	54.5	835
Orel obl.	54.2	844
urban	54.1	850
rural	54.5	835
Ryazan' obl.	54.3	840
urban	53.7	863
rural	55.6	799
Smolensk obl.	54.2	846
urban	53.7	862
rural	55.1	813
Tula obl.	54.6	831
urban	54.5	833
rural	54.9	822
Yaroslavl' obl.	54.5	835
urban	54.4	837
rural	54.9	822
Volgo-Vyatka region	**54.1**	**849**
urban	**53.8**	**857**
rural	**54.6**	**831**
Mari ASSR	53.5	870
urban	54.0	853
rural	52.7	897
Mordvin ASSR	54.3	840
urban	54.1	847
rural	54.6	832
Chuvash ASSR	54.0	852
urban	53.2	878
rural	55.0	818
Nizhnii Novgorod (Gor'kii) obl.	54.5	833
urban	54.2	844
rural	55.6	798

Kirov obl.	53.3	876
urban	53.1	882
rural	53.7	863
Central Black-earth region	**54.4**	**838**
urban	**53.8**	**859**
rural	**55.3**	**807**
Belgorod obl.	54.6	832
urban	53.5	868
rural	56.4	773
Voronezh obl.	54.5	835
urban	53.9	855
rural	55.4	804
Kursk obl.	54.4	839
urban	53.9	856
rural	55.0	817
Lipetsk obl.	54.1	850
urban	53.3	877
rural	55.3	807
Tambov obl.	54.4	837
urban	54.4	837
rural	54.5	836
Volga region	**53.4**	**872**
urban	**53.5**	**868**
rural	**53.1**	**883**
Kalmyk ASSR	51.0	960
urban	52.9	890
rural	49.4	1023
Tatar ASSR	53.6	865
urban	53.4	873
rural	54.3	842
Astrakhan' obl.	52.4	908
urban	53.3	877
rural	50.6	978
Volgograd obl.	53.4	873
urban	53.7	864
rural	52.5	904
Samara (Kuibyshev) obl.	53.6	864
urban	53.9	856
rural	52.6	900

	Women as % of population	Men per 1000 women
Volga region (*cont.*)		
Penza obl.	54.0	851
urban	53.8	857
rural	54.3	841
Saratov obl.	53.3	876
urban	53.4	871
rural	52.9	889
Ul'yanovsk obl.	53.4	873
urban	53.1	884
rural	54.1	847
North Caucasus region	**53.5**	**870**
urban	**53.7**	**861**
rural	**53.1**	**882**
Dagestan ASSR	52.8	893
urban	52.2	915
rural	53.3	877
Kabardino-Balkar ASSR	53.1	883
urban	53.5	870
rural	52.5	904
North Osetiya ASSR	53.7	862
urban	54.0	850
rural	53.0	887
Checheno-Ingush ASSR	53.0	886
urban	53.9	854
rural	52.4	910
Krasnodar krai	53.8	860
urban	54.0	852
rural	53.5	868
incl. Adyge AO	54.1	849
urban	54.6	831
rural	53.5	869
Stavropol' krai	53.4	874
urban	54.1	849
rural	52.5	905

incl. Karachaevo-Cherkess AO	53.1	885
urban	53.4	873
rural	52.5	896
Rostov obl.	53.6	866
urban	53.6	864
rural	53.5	869
Ural' region	**53.1**	**882**
urban	**53.4**	**874**
rural	**52.5**	**904**
Bashkir ASSR	53.0	885
urban	53.1	883
rural	52.9	890
Udmurt ASSR	53.5	869
urban	53.8	859
rural	52.8	893
Kurgan obl.	53.4	873
urban	53.9	857
rural	52.9	892
Orenburg obl.	52.9	890
urban	53.5	871
rural	51.9	926
Perm' obl.	52.8	894
urban	52.8	893
rural	52.7	897
incl. Komi-Permyak AOk	53.3	876
urban	54.9	822
rural	52.7	899
Sverdlovsk obl.	53.4	874
urban	53.6	865
rural	51.6	937
Chelyabinsk obl.	53.2	880
urban	53.3	875
rural	52.5	905
West Siberia region	**52.2**	**916**
urban	**52.4**	**910**
rural	**51.7**	**934**
Altai krai	52.9	892
urban	53.2	879
rural	52.4	909

	Women as % of population	Men per 1000 women
West Siberia region (*cont.*)		
Altai krai (*cont.*)		
incl. Gorno-Altai AO	52.4	910
urban	54.1	849
rural	51.7	933
Kemerovo obl.	52.5	906
urban	52.5	903
rural	51.9	925
Novosibirsk obl.	53.3	876
urban	53.7	861
rural	52.1	920
Omsk obl.	53.0	888
urban	53.5	871
rural	51.9	926
Tomsk obl.	51.3	950
urban	51.5	940
rural	50.7	972
Tyumen' obl.	50.0	1000
urban	49.9	1003
rural	50.3	989
incl. Khanty-Mansi AOk	48.7	1052
urban	48.8	1049
rural	48.0	1084
and Yamalo-Nenets AOk	47.6	1100
urban	47.7	1095
rural	47.2	1120
East Siberia region	**51.3**	**948**
urban	**51.9**	**928**
rural	**50.1**	**998**
Buryat ASSR	51.4	945
urban	51.9	927
rural	50.6	975
Tuva ASSR	50.9	963
urban	51.3	950
rural	50.6	975

Krasnoyarsk krai	51.4	945
urban	52.0	922
rural	49.8	1010
incl. Khakass AO	51.3	949
urban	51.1	958
rural	51.9	927
and Taimyr		
(Dolgano-Nenets) AOk	48.6	1059
urban	49.3	1028
rural	47.1	1122
and Evenki AOk	47.6	1102
urban	49.4	1026
rural	46.8	1138
Irkutsk obl.	51.6	939
urban	52.0	924
rural	49.9	1003
incl. Ust-Ordynskii		
Buryat AOk	50.6	975
urban	51.8	931
rural	50.4	986
Chita obl.	50.8	970
urban	51.1	957
rural	50.1	995
incl. Aginskii-Buryat AOk	50.3	990
urban	50.2	992
rural	50.3	989
Far East region	**49.9**	**1005**
urban	**50.2**	**990**
rural	**48.7**	**1051**
Yakut ASSR	49.6	1017
urban	49.4	1023
rural	49.9	1005
Primor'e krai	50.4	983
urban	50.8	969
rural	49.2	1035
Khabarovsk krai	50.4	984
urban	51.0	960
rural	48.1	1078

	Women as % of population	Men per 1000 women
Far East region (*cont.*)		
Khabarovsk krai (*cont.*)		
incl. Jewish AO	51.1	955
urban	51.8	930
rural	49.9	1005
Amur obl.	50.1	998
urban	50.7	970
rural	48.6	1059
Kamchatka obl.	47.9	1089
urban	47.7	1098
rural	48.8	1049
incl. Koryak AOk	48.4	1067
urban	48.4	1068
rural	48.4	1067
Magadan obl.	48.1	1077
urban	48.8	1050
rural	45.5	1197
incl. Chukot AOk	47.4	1109
urban	47.2	1117
rural	47.9	1088
Sakhalin obl.	49.8	1008
urban	50.0	1001
rural	49.0	1042
Kaliningrad obl.	52.0	924
urban	52.2	916
rural	51.1	956

* Includes outlying settlements which are administratively subordinate to the city.

Source: *Chislennost' naseleniya RSFSR*, s. 75–96.

Women as percentage of students in higher and specialised secondary educational institutions, 1960/1–1990/1
(start of academic year)

	1960/1	1970/1	1980/81	1985/6	1988/9	1990/1
Specialised secondary education	49	56	58	59	58	58
Higher education	45	51	53	56	55	51

Sources: *Narodnoe obrazovanie*, s. 196, 227; *Vestnik statistiki*, 1992, 1, s. 63.

Women doctors*, 1970–90 (end of year)

Year	Thousands	% of all doctors
1970	285	75
1980	407	73
1985	465	72
1986	480	72
1987	472	70
1988	472	69
1989	478	69
1990	475	68

* Includes two categories of dentist. [Ed.]

Sources: *Nar. khoz. RSFSR 1988*, s. 218; *Nar. khoz. RSFSR 1990*, s. 275.

Women teachers in general education day schools*, 1990/1
(start of academic year)

	Thousands	*% of all teachers*
Total**	**1283.7**	**83.1**
Primary school heads	0.5	81.4
Heads of incomplete secondary schools	15.1	55.4
Secondary school heads	32.0	50.5
Deputy heads of incomplete secondary schools	5.7	88.6
Deputy heads of secondary schools	69.2	90.6
Teachers of classes:		
1–4	339.4	98.7
5–11/12	613.3	87.7
Teachers of music and singing, fine art, drawing, physical culture and work training	208.5	48.5

* Schools subordinate to the Ministry of Education (i.e. excluding schools under the aegis of other government departments).
** Persons holding second, part-time, posts are counted only once.

Source: Nar. khoz. RSFSR 1990, s. 240.

Women managers

Among the managers of enterprises and organisations women accounted for 6.5 per cent of the total at the start of each of the following years: 1989, 1990 and 1991. The economic sectors covered include: industry, agriculture, construction and communications.

Source: Vestnik statistiki, 1992, 1, s. 64.

Women blue- and white-collar workers, 1970–90*

Year	Thousands	As % of total
1970	28 585	53
1980	34 314	52
1985	35 138	52
1989	33 927	52
1990	33 481	52

* Annual average numbers.

Sources: *Zhenshchiny v SSSR 1991*, s. 13–14; *Vestnik statistiki*, 1992, 1, s. 63–4.

Women as percentage of collective farm workers, 1970–89*

Year	As % of total
1970	49
1980	44
1985	41
1986	40
1987	39
1988	40
1989	39

* Annual average numbers for workers engaged in the common economy of collective farms, excluding workers in fishery collectives.

Sources: *Nar. khoz. SSSR 1988*, s. 43; *Zhenshchiny v SSSR 1991*, s. 15.

Women specialists* with higher and specialised secondary education employed in the national economy, 1980–9**
(thousands)

	1980	*1985*	*1987*	*1989*
All specialists	16 546	19 086	20 157	20 583
Women	10 139	11 849	12 577	12 857
With higher education				
All	6 710	7 938	8 468	8 685
Women	3 698	4 451	4 769	4 914
With specialised secondary edcucation				
All	9 836	11 148	11 689	11 898
Women	6 441	7 398	7 808	7 943

* Russian: *spetsialisty*. ** The data were collected in a return made in mid-November of each year.

Source: *Nar. khoz. RSFSR 1990*, s. 114.

Female unemployment

At 1 November 1991 a total of 51 400 persons were classified as unemployed at the offices of the Employment Service; women accounted for 66 per cent. The total number receiving unemployment benefit was 7800, of whom 82 per cent were women.

Source: *Statisticheskii press-byulleten' 1992*, 1, s. 42.

At 1 July 1992 the number of persons on the registers at offices of the Employment Service was 779 900, of whom 202 900 were classified as unemployed. Out of the second category over two-thirds were women.

Source: *Ekonomika i zhizn'*, 1992, 30, s. 5.

Percentage of women among blue- and white-collar workers: by economic regions and major territorial-administrative divisions, 1980–90

	1980	1985	1990
Russian SFSR	**52**	**52**	**52**
Northern region	**50**	**50**	**50**
Karelian ASSR	52	51	51
Komi ASSR	49	50	49
Arkhangel'sk obl.	50	48	48
Vologda obl.	51	51	51
Murmansk obl.	52	53	52
North-west region	**56**	**54**	**55**
St. Petersburg (Leningrad)	55	55	56
Leningrad obl.	53	53	54
Novgorod obl.	53	52	53
Pskov obl.	54	53	54
Central region	**54**	**54**	**54**
Bryansk obl.	53	52	52
Vladimir obl.	54	54	53
Ivanovo obl.	55	54	54
Tver' (Kalinin) obl.	54	53	52
Kaluga obl.	53	54	54
Kostroma obl.	52	51	52
Moscow	56	56	56
Moscow obl.	55	55	55
Orel obl.	53	52	51
Ryazan' obl.	53	52	52
Smolensk obl.	53	52	52
Tula obl.	53	53	53
Yaroslavl' obl.	54	53	53
Volgo-Vyatka region	**53**	**53**	**53**
Mari ASSR	53	53	53
Mordvin ASSR	53	53	53

	1980	1985	1990
Volgo Vyatka region (*cont.*)			
Chuvash ASSR	55	54	53
Nizhnii Novgorod (Gor'kii) obl.	53	53	53
Kirov obl.	53	52	52
Central Black-earth region	**52**	**51**	**52**
Belgorod obl.	51	51	51
Voronezh obl.	52	52	52
Kursk obl.	52	51	51
Lipetsk obl.	52	51	51
Tambov obl.	52	51	51
Volga region	**52**	**51**	**52**
Kalmyk ASSR	47	47	49
Tatar ASSR	52	52	52
Astrakhan' obl.	51	50	50
Volgograd obl.	51	51	51
Samara (Kuibyshev) obl.	52	52	52
Penza obl.	51	51	52
Saratov obl.	51	51	53
Ul'yanovsk obl.	53	51	52
North Caucasus region	**51**	**51**	**53**
Dagestan ASSR	51	52	53
Kabardino-Balkar ASSR	51	51	53
North Osetiya ASSR	54	54	57
Checheno-Ingush ASSR	51	53	53
Krasnodar krai	52	52	53
Stavropol krai	50	50	53
Rostov obl.	51	51	52
Ural' region	**53**	**52**	**52**
Bashkir ASSR	52	52	52
Udmurt ASSR	55	54	54
Kurgan obl.	52	52	52
Orenburg obl.	51	51	51
Perm' obl.	53	53	52

Sverdlovsk obl.	53	53	53
Chelyabinsk obl.	52	52	52
West Siberia region	**50**	**49**	**50**
Altai krai	50	49	50
Kemerovo obl.	50	50	51
Novosibirsk obl.	52	52	52
Omsk obl.	51	51	52
Tomsk obl.	50	50	50
Tyumen' obl.	47	46	47
East Siberia region	**51**	**50**	**50**
Buryat ASSR	51	50	52
Tuva ASSR	50	49	53
Krasnoyarsk krai	51	49	50
Irkutsk obl.	51	51	51
Chita obl.	50	50	50
Far East region	**50**	**49**	**50**
Yakut ASSR	48	47	48
Primor'e krai	50	50	51
Khabarovsk krai	51	50	51
Amur obl.	50	50	50
Kamchatka obl.	48	49	50
Magadan obl.	49	49	50
Sakhalin obl.	50	50	51
Kaliningrad obl.	54	54	54

Source: *Sotsial'noe razvitie RSFSR 1990, Tom I*, s. 85–88.

Average time spent per 24 hours on various activities by male and female blue- and white-collar workers, 1990
(in hours and minutes)

	Men		Women	
	Working day	Free day	Working day	Free day
Working	8.12	—	7.58	—
Work-related*	1.30	—	1.20	—
Domestic	1.12	2.51	3.27	6.40
Shopping and obtaining services	0.13	0.34	0.39	0.56
Housework	0.59	2.17	2.48	5.44
Personal enterprise, work on own land	0.19	0.55	0.07	0.23
Children's education	0.28	0.50	0.33	0.52
Free time**	2.51	7.13	1.21	4.37
Meeting physiological needs***	9.07	10.44	9.02	10.42
Other	0.21	1.27	0.12	0.46

* Includes travel, meal breaks etc. ** Includes time spent by parents with children on walks, visits to the cinema and theatre, watching television etc. *** Includes sleep, eating, care of oneself.

Source: *Nar. khoz. RSFSR 1990*, s. 122.

Average time spent per 24 hours on various activities by male and female collective farm workers, 1990
(in hours and minutes)

	Men		Women	
	Working day	*Free day*	*Working day*	*Free day*
Working	7.52	—	7.22	—
Work-related*	0.46	—	0.45	—
Domestic	1.24	3.04	4.09	7.16
Shopping and obtaining services	0.06	0.14	0.28	0.33
Housework	1.18	2.50	3.41	6.43
Personal enterprise, work on own land	1.32	2.23	1.05	1.39
Children's education	0.22	0.39	0.32	0.47
Free time**	2.27	5.34	1.04	3.12
Meeting physiological needs***	9.16	10.47	8.54	10.24
Other	0.21	1.33	0.09	0.42

* Includes travel, meal breaks etc. ** Includes time spent by parents with children on walks, visits to the cinema and theatre, watching television etc. *** Includes sleep, eating, care of oneself.

Note: This and the previous table derive from data collected in March 1990 from a total of 47 000 families of blue- and white-collar workers and collective farm workers.

Source: *Nar. khoz. RSFSR 1990*, s. 122.

**Average time spent per day on domestic activities by male and
female blue- and white-collar industrial workers, 1985
(in hours and minutes)**

	Men		Women	
	Working day	*Free day*	*Working day*	*Free day*
Average per person in 24 hours	0.59	2.44	3.11	6.13
Shopping and obtaining services	0.15	0.58	0.46	1.26
Housework includes:	0.44	1.46	2.25	4.47
Preparing food	0.12	0.21	1.11	1.56
Care of dwelling, furniture, equipment	0.10	0.34	0.23	0.55
Washing, sewing, care of clothes, linen, shoes	0.04	0.11	0.32	1.20
Care of children	0.09	0.15	0.14	0.26
Other forms of housework	0.09	0.25	0.05	0.10

Source: *Nar. khoz. RSFSR 1988*, s. 57.

**Average time spent per day on domestic activities by male and
female collective farm workers, 1985**
(in hours and minutes)

| | Men | | Women | |
	Working day	Free day	Working day	Free day
Average per person in 24 hours	0.45	2.05	3.49	6.23
Shopping and obtaining services	0.07	0.24	0.32	0.48
Housework includes:	0.38	1.41	3.17	5.35
Preparing food	0.10	0.18	1.35	2.05
Care of dwelling, furniture, equipment	0.04	0.13	0.33	0.58
Washing, sewing, care of clothes, linen, shoes	0.02	0.07	0.41	1.37
Care of children	0.07	0.17	0.21	0.34
Other forms of housework	0.15	0.46	0.07	0.21

Note: This and the previous table derive from data collected in March
1985 from a total of 27 500 families of blue- and white-collar workers
and collective farm workers.

Source: *Nar. khoz. RSFSR 1988*, s. 57.

Abortions, 1980–1990

	Thousands	Per 1000 women aged 15–49	Per 100 births*
1980	4342	118.0	201.2
1981	4237	115.7	
1982	4299	117.5	
1983	4178	114.3	
1984	4209	114.8	
1985	4258	115.7	180.1
1986	4362	118.6	
1987	4166	113.9	
1988**	4402	121.2	191.5
1989	4242	117.5	200.2
1990	3920	95.8	200.8

* Includes still-births. ** From 1988 the total includes mini-abortions, i.e. those performed in the early period of pregnancy by means of the vacuum-aspiration method. They numbered 570 000 in 1988, 824 000 in 1989 and 952 000 in 1990.

Sources: Nar. khoz. RSFSR 1988, s. 242; *Nar. khoz. RSFSR 1990*, s. 266.

Notes: These data relate only to abortions performed in units which formed part of the system controlled by the USSR Ministry of Health, and thus exclude those performed in other state-owned units, particularly those run by the Ministry of Rail Transport. What appear to be complete totals are available for the years 1980 and 1985; the figures were 4506 and 4552 respectively. They yield rates of 122.8 and 123.6 per 100 000 women aged 15–49. (*Source: Naselenie SSSR 1987*, s. 319.)

It should be added that the data refer only to legal abortions. In 1990, in the former USSR as a whole 172 persons were convicted of performing illegal abortions; out of that total, 91 persons had repeated the offence and had caused serious consequences for the patient.

The former USSR was the only developed country where the limitation of family size was achieved by means of abortion to a far greater extent than by contraception. In 1987 a large survey of pregnant women found that amongst respondents in the Russian Federation 6.0 per cent said they had not heard of contraceptive devices and a further 56.8 per cent said they did not use them. Women who stated that they used them regularly made up 21.8 per cent of the total, while 9.7 per cent used them occasionally.

Quite apart from the shortages of female contraceptive devices, caused by inadequate production and distribution, women were deterred from using them by having first to negotiate a complicated official procedure. In the Russian Federation as many as 12.0 per cent of respondents complained that female contraceptives were difficult to obtain. (*Source*: *Vestnik statistiki*, 1991, 8, s. 58, 60–2.)

Maternal mortality*, 1980–9

	1980	1985	1989
Absolute numbers	1498	1282	1059
Per 100 000 births	68.0	54.0	49.0

* Due to complications of pregnancy, birth and the postnatal period.

'The level of maternal mortality in the USSR is 2.8–5 times higher than in Japan, France, the Federal Republic of Germany, Great Britain, and the USA. [In 1989 the all-Union rate was 43.8 per 100 000 births.]'

'With the object of further improving the conditions of work for women, a review is being provided for in 1990–91 of the Lists of productive processes, occupations and jobs with heavy and harmful work conditions in which the use of female and adolescent labour is forbidden; the Lists are being supplemented with the types of job to which women of child-bearing age must not be recruited.'

Source: *Zhenshchiny v SSSR 1991*, s. 38.

8   Education

Level of educational attainment of population aged 15 and over per 1000 population, at censuses of 1979 and 1989

	1979	1989
Total population		
Completed higher	77	113
Incomplete higher	17	17
Specialised secondary	127	192
General secondary	204	274
Incomplete secondary	272	210
All higher and secondary	697	806
Urban population		
Completed higher	98	136
Incomplete higher	21	21
Specialised secondary	147	212
General secondary	236	287
Incomplete secondary	268	198
All higher and secondary	770	854
Rural population		
Completed higher	28	47
Incomplete higher	6	7
Specialised secondary	79	134
General secondary	130	237
Incomplete secondary	282	243
All higher and secondary	525	668

Source: *Sotsial'noe razvitie naseleniya RSFSR 1990, Tom II*, s. 27–8.

Level of educational attainment of employed population per 1000 population, at censuses of 1979 and 1989

	1979	*1989*
Total population		
Completed higher	101	146
Incomplete higher	12	13
Specialised secondary	164	242
General secondary	243	336
Incomplete secondary	283	178
All higher and secondary	803	915
Urban population		
Completed higher	124	170
Incomplete higher	13	15
Specialised secondary	184	260
General secondary	266	337
Incomplete secondary	268	156
All higher and secondary	855	938
Rural population		
Completed higher	41	67
Incomplete higher	7	8
Specialised secondary	112	185
General secondary	182	333
Incomplete secondary	324	250
All higher and secondary	666	843

Source: *Sotsial'noe razvitie naseleniya RSFSR 1990, Tom II*, s. 29.

Level of educational attainment of men aged 15 and over per 1000 male population, at censuses of 1979 and 1989

	1979	1989
Total population		
Higher	84	117
Incomplete higher and secondary*	353	506
Incomplete secondary	318	231
All higher and secondary	755	854
Urban population		
Higher	106	141
Incomplete higher and secondary*	403	538
Incomplete secondary	308	214
All higher and secondary	817	893
Rural population		
Higher	32	48
Incomplete higher and secondary*	234	417
Incomplete secondary	344	279
All higher and secondary	610	744

* Specialised secondary and general secondary.

Source: *Sotsial'noe razvitie naseleniya RSFSR 1990, Tom II*, s. 39.

Level of educational attainment of women aged 15 and over per 1000 female population, at censuses of 1979 and 1989

	1979	1989
Total population		
Higher	71	110
Incomplete higher and secondary*	344	464
Incomplete secondary	235	192
All higher and secondary	650	766
Urban population		
Higher	91	132
Incomplete higher and secondary*	406	506
Incomplete secondary	236	185
All higher and secondary	733	823
Rural population		
Higher	25	45
Incomplete higher and secondary*	200	345
Incomplete secondary	232	213
All higher and secondary	457	603

* Specialised secondary and general secondary.

Source: *Sotsial'noe razvitie naseleniya RSFSR 1990, Tom II*, s. 39.

Social Trends in Contemporary Russia

Level of educational attainment of population aged 15 and over: by economic regions and major territorial-administrative divisions, at 1989 census

Key to columns: 1 Higher
2 Incomplete higher
3 Specialised secondary
4 General secondary
5 Incomplete secondary

	1	2	3	4	5
(Per 1000 population aged 15 and over)					
Russian SFSR	**113**	**17**	**192**	**274**	**210**
Northern region	**97**	**12**	**209**	**289**	**229**
Karelian ASSR	96	14	200	271	239
Komi ASSR	89	12	215	332	224
Arkhangel'sk obl.	88	12	201	263	260
incl. Nenets AOk	89	10	228	276	259
Vologda obl.	82	12	194	251	235
Murmansk obl.	139	12	238	335	176
North-west region	**165**	**27**	**213**	**264**	**184**
St. Petersburg (Leningrad)*	213	37	227	265	162
Leningrad obl.	94	11	202	274	225
Novgorod obl.	88	11	181	245	227
Pskov obl.	81	10	173	256	205
Central region	**155**	**21**	**195**	**251**	**202**
Bryansk obl.	77	12	172	263	211
Vladimir obl.	92	12	172	284	228
Ivanovo obl.	89	16	183	255	236
Tver' (Kalinin) obl.	88	13	201	234	228
Kaluga obl.	111	12	204	260	208
Kostroma obl.	83	14	193	230	220
Moscow*	264	35	199	248	156
Moscow obl.	148	18	209	253	210

Orel obl.	88	13	171	263	227
Ryazan' obl.	87	16	183	246	225
Smolensk obl.	87	14	196	233	242
Tula obl.	93	11	181	241	238
Yaroslavl' obl.	95	15	186	263	226
Volgo-Vyatka region	**89**	**14**	**170**	**283**	**212**
Mari ASSR	97	16	165	304	211
Mordvin ASSR	88	17	164	321	165
Chuvash ASSR	79	13	163	311	231
Nizhnii Novgorod (Gor'kii) obl.	96	14	175	266	212
Kirov obl.	79	11	168	269	224
Central Black-earth region	**89**	**14**	**170**	**268**	**193**
Belgorod obl.	83	13	181	274	181
Voronezh obl.	104	17	162	280	180
Kursk obl.	79	13	160	269	203
Lipetsk obl.	84	12	182	263	209
Tambov obl.	80	13	173	245	207
Volga region	**100**	**17**	**188**	**282**	**207**
Kalmyk ASSR	92	18	190	300	186
Tatar ASSR	95	16	163	320	208
Astrakhan' obl.	97	15	229	258	197
Volgograd obl.	97	16	197	286	199
Samara (Kuibyshev) obl.	112	18	207	277	204
Penza obl.	88	13	169	259	210
Saratov obl.	110	21	187	258	222
Ul'yanovsk obl.	89	14	181	279	204
North Caucasus region	**97**	**16**	**184**	**272**	**212**
Dagestan ASSR	83	17	157	284	219
Kabardino-Balkar ASSR	101	19	197	296	204
North Osetiya ASSR	133	29	199	280	190
Checheno-Ingush ASSR	76	17	148	294	215
Krasnodar krai	92	13	184	269	215
incl. Adyge AO	91	13	190	278	206
Stavropol' krai	96	15	182	276	202
incl. Karachaevo-Cherkess AO	96	16	167	306	190
Rostov obl.	106	17	200	259	215

	1	2	3	4	5
Ural' region	**84**	**13**	**180**	**289**	**229**
Bashkir ASSR	76	13	170	306	223
Udmurt ASSR	92	14	164	318	219
Kurgan obl.	72	12	168	259	232
Orenburg obl.	79	13	191	273	228
Perm' obl.	80	13	173	273	250
incl. Komi-Permyak AOk	43	7	153	180	308
Sverdlovsk obl.	91	14	187	288	231
Chelyabinsk obl.	90	14	192	291	216
West Siberia region	**96**	**16**	**201**	**279**	**210**
Altai krai	82	13	181	261	216
incl. Gorno-Altai AO	80	16	170	265	232
Kemerovo obl.	80	13	198	271	227
Novosibirsk obl.	117	19	193	244	222
Omsk obl.	97	18	183	289	206
Tomsk obl.	116	27	199	279	196
Tyumen' obl.	102	15	248	330	180
incl. Khanty-Mansi AOk	104	10	276	399	150
and Yamalo-Nenets AOk	125	12	292	386	134
East Siberia region	**100**	**17**	**197**	**276**	**226**
Buryat ASSR	118	18	188	287	208
Tuva ASSR	79	16	183	295	253
Krasnoyarsk krai	95	16	201	280	216
incl. Khakass AO	80	13	195	273	226
and Taimyr					
(Dolgano-Nenets) AOk	110	13	254	386	154
and Evenki AOk	116	15	266	326	184
Irkutsk obl.	101	18	199	271	240
incl. Ust'-Ordynskii					
Buryat AOk	71	10	134	268	271
Chita obl.	103	12	192	266	234
incl. Aginskii-Buryat AOk	99	11	156	309	236

Far East region	125	17	225	300	210
Yakut ASSR	113	17	230	377	162
Primor'e krai	128	18	216	278	222
Khabarovsk krai	127	18	219	264	237
incl. Jewish AO	77	8	205	228	299
Amur obl.	112	15	215	263	233
Kamchatka obl.	155	14	254	350	167
incl. Koryak AOk	107	11	248	356	181
Magadan obl.	139	17	258	367	168
incl. Chukot AOk	149	17	275	374	144
Sakhalin obl.	112	12	236	323	196
Kaliningrad obl.	124	16	225	280	206

* The figure includes outlying settlements which are administratively subordinate to the city.

Source: *Kratkaya kharakteristika naseleniya RSFSR, Chast' I*, s. 158–68.

Pupils taught in Russian and languages of other nationalities of the republic in day general education schools, 1980/1–1990/1*

Language	1980/1	1986/7	1990/1
	(Thousands)		
Russian	16 832	18 320	19 599
Bashkir	68	55	50
Buryat	6	6	17
Languages of the peoples of Dagestan	56	52	40
Komi-Permyak	1	0.2	0.04
Mari	14	11	13
Mordva	12	5	5
Tatar	217	108	98
Tuva	38	30	32
Udmurt	2	2	1
Chechen	1	0.2	12
Chuvash	58	44	37
Yakut	46	37	48
	(As percentage of all pupils)		
Russian	97.0	98.1	98.1
Bashkir	0.4	0.3	0.25
Buryat	0.04	0.03	0.1
Languages of the peoples of Dagestan	0.3	0.3	0.2
Komi-Permyak	0.00	0.00	0.00
Mari	0.1	0.06	0.07
Mordva	0.1	0.02	0.02
Tatar	1.3	0.6	0.5
Tuva	0.2	0.2	0.16
Udmurt	0.01	0.01	0.007
Chechen	0.01	0.00	0.06
Chuvash	0.3	0.24	0.019
Yakut	0.3	0.2	0.24

* At start of academic year, excluding pupils in schools for mentally and physically handicapped children.

Sources: *Sotsial'noe razvitya SSSR*, s. 225; *Vestnik statistiki*, 1991, 12, s. 48.

Note: In rendering a few of the names of languages, I have followed the conventions used by Bernard Comrie in *The Languages of the Soviet Union* (C.U.P., 1981). [Ed.]

Pupils taught in Russian and languages of other nationalities in evening (shift) general education schools, at start of academic year 1990/1

Language	Thousands	As % of all pupils
Russian	521	99.6
Bashkir	0.2	0.04
Tatar	1	0.2
Tuva	0.5	0.1
Chuvash	0.04	0.01
Yakut	0.2	0.03

Source: *Vestnik statistiki*, 1991, 12, s. 50.

Students in specialised secondary and higher educational establishments taught in Russian and languages of other nationalities, at start of academic year 1990/1

| | Secondary specialised | | Higher | |
	(Thousands)	(As %)	(Thousands)	(As %)
Russian	2261	99.6	2792	98.8
Abaza	1	0.03	—	—
Altai	0.1	0.01	—	—
Ingush	—	—	0.03	0.00
Komi-Permyak	0.1	0.01	—	—
Tatar	2	0.1	2	0.1
Chechen	—	—	0.1	0.00
Chuvash	0.1	0.00	1	0.02
Yakut	0.4	0.02	—	—

Source: *Vestnik statistiki*, 1991, 12, s. 53.

Percentage of main nationalities of autonomous areas aged 15 and over with higher and incomplete higher education, at censuses of 1979 and 1989

	Higher		*Incomplete higher*	
	1979	*1989*	*1979*	*1989*
RSFSR	**7.7**	**11.3**	**1.7**	**1.7**
Russians	7.7	11.5	1.7	1.7
Bashkir ASSR	**5.0**	**7.6**	**1.3**	**1.3**
Bashkirs	3.8	6.9	1.2	1.4
Russians	6.1	8.7	1.3	1.3
Buryat ASSR	**7.3**	**11.8**	**1.7**	**1.8**
Buryats	11.5	18.3	3.1	3.2
Russians	5.9	9.5	1.2	1.4
Dagestan ASSR	**5.6**	**8.3**	**1.7**	**1.7**
Avars	4.2	6.6	1.5	1.6
Aguls	4.7	8.4	1.4	2.1
Dargwa	4.0	6.4	1.5	1.5
Kumyks	5.3	8.2	1.8	1.7
Lakk	9.2	13.4	2.8	2.9
Lezghi	6.0	9.2	1.9	1.8
Nogais	3.5	7.2	1.6	1.4
Rutuls	3.8	6.7	1.5	1.5
Tabasaran	3.8	6.7	1.3	1.4
Tsakhurs	4.6	8.7	1.5	1.7
Russians	8.6	12.4	1.9	1.9
Kabardino-Balkar ASSR	**7.3**	**10.1**	**1.5**	**1.9**
Kabarda	6.0	8.6	1.5	2.0
Balkars	6.9	10.8	2.1	2.6
Russians	8.4	11.3	1.2	1.5
Kalmyk ASSR	**5.6**	**9.2**	**1.5**	**1.8**
Kalmyks	6.1	12.0	2.0	2.7
Russians	5.8	7.9	1.2	1.3

Karelian ASSR	**6.4**	**9.6**	**1.4**	**1.4**
Karelians	3.4	5.9	1.0	1.0
Russians	7.4	10.7	1.6	1.5
Komi ASSR	**6.1**	**8.9**	**1.2**	**1.2**
Komi	4.5	7.1	1.1	1.0
Russians	7.2	10.1	1.3	1.3
Mari ASSR	**6.0**	**9.7**	**1.7**	**1.6**
Mariitsy	3.4	6.2	1.0	1.2
Russians	8.2	12.7	2.2	1.9
Mordvin ASSR	**5.3**	**8.8**	**1.5**	**1.7**
Mordvinians	3.7	7.1	1.3	1.5
Russians	6.2	9.9	1.7	1.8
North Osetiya ASSR	**9.4**	**13.3**	**2.9**	**2.9**
Ossetes	9.4	13.7	2.9	2.9
Russians	10.0	14.1	2.9	2.5
Tatar ASSR	**6.4**	**9.5**	**1.7**	**1.6**
Tatars	5.0	8.3	1.5	1.5
Russians	7.8	10.9	1.8	1.8
Tuva ASSR	**5.4**	**7.9**	**1.3**	**1.6**
Tuvinians	3.9	6.1	1.2	1.5
Russians	6.8	10.3	1.4	1.6
Udmurt ASSR	**6.0**	**9.2**	**1.3**	**1.4**
Udmurts	3.2	5.7	1.1	1.1
Russians	7.5	11.0	1.5	1.5
Checheno-Ingush ASSR	**5.3**	**7.6**	**1.4**	**1.7**
Chechens	2.2	4.4	0.9	1.4
Ingush	3.4	5.7	1.3	2.1
Russians	9.2	13.6	1.9	1.9
Chuvash ASSR	**5.1**	**7.9**	**1.2**	**1.3**
Chuvash	3.8	6.5	1.1	1.2
Russians	8.1	11.3	1.4	1.5

	Higher		Incomplete higher	
	1979	*1989*	*1979*	*1989*
Yakut ASSR	**7.9**	**11.3**	**1.4**	**1.7**
Yakuts	7.2	11.9	1.7	2.1
Russians	8.2	11.3	1.2	1.5
Adyge AO	**6.1**	**9.1**	**1.1**	**1.3**
Adyge	8.2	12.0	1.6	1.6
Russians	5.4	8.2	1.0	1.2
Gorno-Altai AO	**5.0**	**8.0**	**1.5**	**1.6**
Altais	4.6	7.8	1.1	1.5
Russians	5.1	7.9	1.6	1.6
Jewish AO	**5.1**	**7.7**	**0.6**	**0.8**
Jews	8.4	13.4	1.1	1.0
Russians	4.8	7.4	0.6	0.7
Karachaevo-Cherkess AO	**6.2**	**9.6**	**1.2**	**1.6**
Karachais	7.2	10.5	1.5	2.0
Cherkess	6.5	9.9	1.2	1.6
Russians	5.5	8.8	1.0	1.2
Khakass AO	**4.7**	**8.0**	**1.0**	**1.3**
Khakass	4.9	8.9	1.2	1.5
Russians	4.8	8.1	1.0	1.2
Aginskii-Buryat AOk	**5.7**	**9.9**	**0.9**	**1.1**
Buryats	8.1	13.6	1.2	1.6
Russians	3.2	5.3	0.5	0.5
Komi-Permyak AOk	**2.6**	**4.3**	**0.8**	**0.7**
Komi-Permyaki	1.9	3.7	0.7	0.7
Russians	3.8	5.3	0.9	0.8
Koryak AOk	**8.6**	**10.7**	**1.1**	**1.1**
Koryaki	1.2	3.3	0.4	0.9
Russians	10.2	12.0	1.3	1.1

Nenets AOk	**6.3**	**8.9**	**0.8**	**1.0**
Nentsy	2.3	3.3	0.4	0.5
Russians	6.9	9.8	0.8	1.1
Taimyr				
(Dolgano-Nenets) AOk	**7.8**	**11.0**	**1.1**	**1.3**
Dolgany	2.3	3.9	0.3	0.4
Nenets	1.1	2.1	0.4	0.6
Russians	8.8	12.1	1.2	1.4
Ust'-Ordynskii Buryat AOk	**4.4**	**7.1**	**0.8**	**1.0**
Buryats	8.6	13.5	1.6	1.9
Russians	2.4	3.7	0.4	0.6
Khanty-Mansi AOk	**7.5**	**10.4**	**0.8**	**1.0**
Khanty	2.2	3.4	0.3	0.5
Mansi	2.7	4.4	0.3	0.5
Russians	7.8	11.2	0.8	1.1
Chukot AOk	**10.6**	**14.9**	**1.3**	**1.7**
Chukchi	1.7	3.4	0.4	0.9
Russians	11.4	16.1	1.4	1.8
Evenki AOk	**7.6**	**11.6**	**1.3**	**1.5**
Evenki	4.6	6.8	0.7	1.6
Russians	8.4	12.6	1.4	1.6
Yamalo-Nenets AOk	**8.1**	**12.5**	**0.9**	**1.2**
Nentsy	0.5	1.4	0.2	0.3
Russians	9.9	14.1	1.0	1.3

Source: *Statisticheskii Press-byulleten'*, 1992, 1, s. 103–8.

Percentage of main nationalities of autonomous areas aged 15 and over with various types of secondary education, at censuses of 1979 and 1989

Key to columns: 1–2   Specialised secondary
3–4   General secondary
5–6   Incomplete secondary

	1 1979	2 1989	3 1979	4 1989	5 1979	6 1989
RSFSR	**12.7**	**19.2**	**20.4**	**27.4**	**27.2**	**21.0**
Russians	13.1	19.7	20.3	26.7	27.1	21.2
Bashkir ASSR	**10.3**	**17.0**	**21.0**	**30.6**	**32.9**	**22.3**
Bashkirs	7.1	14.3	20.2	33.8	31.7	22.3
Russians	13.0	19.3	20.9	28.6	28.1	21.8
Buryat ASSR	**12.8**	**18.8**	**20.6**	**28.7**	**28.8**	**20.8**
Buryats	10.5	16.1	24.8	30.4	23.4	16.3
Russians	13.2	19.4	19.1	27.7	30.8	22.7
Dagestan ASSR	**9.4**	**15.7**	**16.6**	**28.4**	**28.3**	**21.9**
Avars	6.6	12.3	16.7	32.2	29.1	22.5
Aguls	7.1	13.9	14.4	27.1	27.3	22.6
Dargwa	5.6	11.2	13.0	26.8	30.6	24.6
Kumyks	10.5	19.1	17.3	27.4	29.0	22.2
Lakk	10.1	18.4	17.2	25.4	27.6	19.8
Lezghi	8.7	15.5	19.2	31.3	29.3	20.0
Nogais	10.8	16.6	13.8	28.1	30.1	23.2
Rutuls	7.1	13.0	16.8	31.7	29.6	20.2
Tabasaran	6.1	10.9	13.5	29.0	34.1	25.1
Tsakhurs	7.2	8.6	16.9	35.5	24.5	16.8
Russians	17.0	24.9	17.9	20.9	22.2	19.0
Kabardino-Balkar ASSR	**12.0**	**19.7**	**22.7**	**29.6**	**26.7**	**20.4**
Kabarda	8.9	17.7	24.8	33.6	28.9	20.8
Balkars	8.8	17.4	22.5	29.8	24.2	17.6
Russians	15.7	23.0	20.5	24.7	25.3	21.0

Kalmyk ASSR	**11.1**	**19.1**	**20.5**	**30.0**	**28.0**	**18.6**
Kalmyks	10.6	20.1	23.0	31.5	24.9	13.3
Russians	12.5	19.9	18.6	26.6	29.0	21.6
Karelian ASSR	**14.5**	**20.0**	**17.8**	**27.1**	**31.5**	**23.9**
Karelians	10.7	15.9	13.1	23.6	30.2	25.0
Russians	16.2	21.6	19.4	28.1	31.8	23.7
Komi ASSR	**16.0**	**21.5**	**22.3**	**33.2**	**33.2**	**22.4**
Komi	13.5	18.9	14.7	24.6	33.6	27.2
Russians	17.6	22.8	24.0	34.3	33.1	21.5
Mari ASSR	**10.9**	**16.5**	**20.0**	**30.4**	**29.1**	**21.1**
Mariitsy	7.2	13.5	18.7	33.3	33.9	23.5
Russians	14.1	19.1	21.0	27.9	25.3	19.2
Mordvin ASSR	**9.8**	**16.4**	**25.1**	**32.1**	**22.4**	**16.5**
Mordvinians	7.0	14.1	23.8	32.2	23.2	16.2
Russians	11.4	17.9	25.5	31.4	21.5	16.4
North Osetiya ASSR	**13.4**	**19.9**	**22.8**	**28.0**	**23.0**	**19.0**
Ossetes	13.1	20.1	23.5	29.0	23.2	18.6
Russians	15.0	21.5	21.0	24.5	22.3	19.3
Tatar ASSR	**10.0**	**16.3**	**23.7**	**32.0**	**28.1**	**20.8**
Tatars	7.8	14.5	23.8	33.3	30.1	21.6
Russians	12.5	18.5	23.8	30.4	26.1	20.0
Tuva ASSR	**11.9**	**18.3**	**20.6**	**29.5**	**29.5**	**25.3**
Tuvinians	7.6	14.4	22.6	34.1	30.0	26.9
Russians	16.9	24.0	17.8	22.1	29.3	23.5
Udmurt ASSR	**10.7**	**16.4**	**22.4**	**31.8**	**28.9**	**21.9**
Udmurts	7.6	13.7	20.1	32.7	32.0	23.5
Russians	12.5	17.9	23.2	30.9	27.2	21.2
Checheno-Ingush ASSR	**9.3**	**14.8**	**18.6**	**29.4**	**27.5**	**21.5**
Chechens	5.0	10.7	19.1	33.8	29.9	22.1
Ingush	6.2	12.2	21.4	32.7	28.1	21.8
Russians	15.5	23.2	17.0	20.3	24.4	20.3

	1 1979	2 1989	3 1979	4 1989	5 1979	6 1989
Chuvash ASSR	**10.3**	**16.3**	**21.5**	**31.1**	**31.3**	**23.1**
Chuvash	8.1	14.1	21.5	32.7	34.2	24.9
Russians	16.2	22.0	21.8	27.7	24.5	19.0
Yakut ASSR	**17.7**	**23.0**	**24.4**	**37.7**	**27.9**	**16.2**
Yakuts	11.8	17.3	24.2	37.4	25.7	15.1
Russians	21.3	25.9	23.6	36.1	29.7	17.8
Adyge AO	**11.8**	**19.0**	**19.8**	**27.8**	**26.0**	**20.6**
Adyge	10.9	19.8	24.9	31.2	22.6	16.1
Russians	12.0	18.9	18.4	26.5	26.9	22.0
Gorno-Altai AO	**11.1**	**17.0**	**16.5**	**26.5**	**28.8**	**23.2**
Altais	9.3	16.9	16.4	28.4	29.6	21.9
Russians	11.7	16.9	16.3	25.2	28.6	24.0
Jewish AO	**13.7**	**20.5**	**17.5**	**22.8**	**34.2**	**29.9**
Jews	19.2	26.4	14.9	17.0	29.0	25.8
Russians	13.5	20.5	17.7	22.5	35.5	30.9
Karachaevo-						
Cherkess AO	**10.2**	**16.7**	**21.8**	**30.6**	**24.7**	**19.0**
Karachais	6.3	12.3	25.6	35.3	21.9	16.4
Cherkess	9.3	16.7	24.5	34.1	27.6	18.8
Russians	12.6	19.3	18.6	26.4	25.5	20.8
Khakass AO	**12.4**	**19.5**	**18.9**	**27.3**	**30.6**	**22.6**
Khakass	7.8	14.5	17.3	28.8	29.8	22.3
Russians	13.3	20.5	19.3	26.9	31.0	23.0
Aginskii-Buryat AOk	**9.4**	**15.6**	**20.0**	**30.9**	**32.1**	**23.6**
Buryats	9.0	15.6	21.3	32.2	28.2	18.6
Russians	9.8	15.5	17.2	29.2	36.4	29.7
Komi-Permyak AOk	**9.5**	**15.3**	**9.0**	**18.0**	**33.0**	**30.8**
Komi-Permyaki	8.4	14.7	7.6	16.7	32.2	29.8
Russians	11.5	16.8	11.2	19.8	34.5	32.8

Koryak AOk	**21.1**	**24.8**	**21.1**	**35.6**	**29.5**	**18.1**
Koryaki	6.5	11.4	13.8	38.9	37.8	24.9
Russians	25.1	28.1	22.8	34.5	28.3	17.6
Nenets AOk	**17.5**	**22.8**	**18.8**	**27.6**	**31.8**	**25.9**
Nentsy	9.4	12.5	8.7	19.4	33.5	38.8
Russians	18.9	24.1	19.4	27.7	32.1	24.9
Taimyr (Dolgano-Nenets) AOk	**20.1**	**25.4**	**27.1**	**38.6**	**26.8**	**15.4**
Dolgany	11.8	15.2	11.0	34.5	28.8	24.1
Nenets	4.8	8.2	8.6	23.8	30.3	30.7
Russians	22.4	27.3	29.7	39.5	26.8	14.2
Ust'-Ordynskii Buryat AOk	**8.4**	**13.4**	**16.2**	**26.8**	**31.1**	**27.1**
Buryats	9.8	15.4	20.9	28.7	28.5	21.9
Russians	7.9	12.4	13.9	25.9	32.7	30.3
Khanty-Mansi AOk	**19.4**	**27.6**	**27.7**	**39.9**	**29.5**	**15.0**
Khanty	10.2	16.5	8.6	22.0	29.5	27.1
Mansi	11.2	18.9	8.8	25.0	34.3	30.3
Russians	20.0	28.1	26.6	36.9	29.8	16.0
Chukot AOk	**23.5**	**27.5**	**29.0**	**37.4**	**25.9**	**14.4**
Chukchi	7.9	11.9	11.7	34.9	30.7	25.4
Russians	25.3	29.0	29.6	36.5	25.9	13.9
Evenki AOk	**19.6**	**26.6**	**19.9**	**32.6**	**27.7**	**18.4**
Evenki	10.5	15.9	14.1	28.4	29.0	28.5
Russians	22.4	28.6	21.0	32.6	27.9	17.3
Yamalo-Nenets AOk	**20.7**	**29.2**	**25.8**	**38.6**	**26.9**	**13.4**
Nentsy	4.1	8.4	6.9	22.6	22.6	24.4
Russians	24.6	31.2	27.9	36.6	27.6	13.8

Source: Statisticheskii Press-byulleten', 1992, 1, s. 109–14.

Schools for mentally and physically handicapped pupils, 1980–90*

	1980/1	1985/6	1990/1
Number of schools			
Total	1576	1655	1817
For:			
Mentally handicapped	1248	1314	1452
Blind	26	24	20
Partially sighted	45	47	51
Deaf/deaf and dumb	93	88	82
Partially deaf and dumb	58	59	70
After poliomyelitis and cerebral paralysis	42	41	40
Severe speech defects	58	63	61
Psychically retarded	4	17	41
Other	2	2	—
Also: forest sanatoria schools	143	131	107
Number of pupils (in thousands)			
Total	269.5	307.0	312.1
Mentally handicapped	213.1	246.8	251.6
Blind	4.6	4.6	3.7
Partially sighted	7.3	7.7	7.8
Deaf/deaf and dumb	15.1	13.9	12.5
Partially deaf	10.7	10.8	11.2
After poliomyelitis and cerebral paralysis	7.3	7.3	6.5
Severe speech defects	10.1	11.8	10.8
Psychically retarded	1.0	3.6	8.0
Other schools	0.3	0.5	—
Also:			
Handicapped pupils in classes in general education schools	3.7	7.9	53.0
Of which:			
Mentally handicapped	—	—	7.1
Psychically retarded	—	—	44.9
At forest sanatoria schools	17.2	15.3	11.6

* At start of school year.

Source: *Narodnoe obrazovanie v RSFSR*, s. 58.

The condition of day general education schools

As a result of the shortage of school accommodation in the Russian Federation, there continues to be an increase in shift-working at day schools for general education. At the start of the school year 1991/2, a total of 21 500 schools (32.5 per cent) operated on a two-shift basis and 658 (1 per cent) on a three-shift basis. In urban areas 70 per cent of the schools were obliged to run two shifts and 3 per cent to run three shifts.

**Distribution of pupils by shift, at start of school years
1985/6–1991/2 (percentages)**

	1985/6	1989/90	1990/91	1991/92
Urban and rural areas				
1st shift	80.7	77.7	76.8	75.7
2nd shift	19.2	22.0	22.8	23.8
3rd shift	0.1	0.3	0.4	0.5
Urban areas				
1st shift	76.4	72.5	71.6	70.3
2nd shift	23.5	27.1	27.9	29.0
3rd shift	0.1	0.4	0.5	0.7
Rural areas				
1st shift	91.2	90.4	89.8	88.8
2nd shift	8.8	9.5	10.1	11.1
3rd shift	0.0	0.1	0.1	0.1

Notes: At the start of the 1991/2 school year, 4.7 million pupils (23.8 per cent) were being taught in the second shift and 100 800 (0.5 per cent) in the third shift. During the past six years the number of school children having lessons in second-shift arrangements increased by 1.2 million, while the numbers in third shifts rose by 82 thousand. The growth in shift-teaching was especially marked in urban schools. There the proportion of pupils learning on the second shift rose from 23.5 per cent in 1985/6 to 29.0 per cent in 1991/2; for the third shift the figures rose from 0.1 to 0.7 per cent.

A high level of shift-working occurred in the schools of the Chechen-Ingush republic (39 per cent of pupils had lessons on the second shift), in Sakhalin, Kamchatka, Kemerovo, Murmansk, Tyumen' and Magadan *oblasti*, and also in Primor'e *krai* (33–35 per cent). There is a shortage of schools in the Khanty-Mansi *okrug* (where 39.5 per cent of children studied on the second shift) and in the Yamalo-Nenets (38.0 per cent), Taimyr (36.3 per cent) and Evenki (28.9 per cent) *okruga*.

Many school buildings are in an unsatisfactory condition. At the start of the 1991/2 school year 30.6 per cent of schools needed capital building work undertaken, 6.2 per cent were in a ruinous condition, and only 39 per cent had all types of amenity. About 25 thousand (37.5 per cent) lacked a supply of piped water, 19 thousand (29 per cent) had no central heating and 32 thousand (48.5 per cent) had no sewerage system.

More than a half of school premises require capital building work or are in a ruinous condition in Murmansk, Astrakhan', Kamchatka and Magadan *oblasti*, in the Chuvash, Kalmyk, Kabardino-Balkar and Buryat republics, and in Stavropol and Primor'e *kraya*.

The material base of rural schools is markedly worse; two-thirds of them do not have a sewerage system, almost a half lack piped water and a third have no central heating. In the Kalmyk, Bashkir, Gorno-Altai and Tuva republics, and in Irkutsk *oblast'*, 60–95 per cent of school buildings in the countryside do not have piped water, central heating or a sewerage system.

Source: *Statisticheskii Press-byulleten'*, 1992, 1, s. 46–7.

Students in specialised secondary and higher educational institutions, 1980/1–1990/1 (start of academic year)

	1980/1	1985/6	1989/90	1990/1
Specialised secondary education				
Students (thousands)	2642	2478	2338	2270
In:				
day departments	1579	1536	1537	1514
evening departments	339	261	184	164
distance learning	724	681	617	592
Students				
per 10 000 population	190	172	158	153
No. of institutions	2505	2566	2595	2603
Higher education				
Students (thousands)	3046	2966	2861	2825
In:				
day departments	1686	1569	1624	1648
evening departments	401	384	311	285
distance learning	959	1013	926	892
Students				
per 10 000 population	219	206	193	190
No. of institutions	494	502	512	514

Source: *Nar. Khoz. RSFSR 1990*, s. 242.

University students and universities, 1980–90

	1980	1985	1989	1990
Students (thousands)				
Total	303.6	294.8	309.2	328.1
No. admitted	59.7	61.1	65.4	68.3
Graduates*	49.5	50.2	44.9	48.0
Universities				
	40	40	40	42

* Russian: *spetsialisty*.

Source: *Nar. khoz. RSFSR 1990*, s. 243.

Students completing specialised secondary and higher education, 1980–90 (thousands)

	1980	1985	1989	1990
Specialised secondary education				
Total	721	659	640	637
In:				
day departments	458	414	407	414
evening departments	78	60	53	50
distance learning	185	185	180	173
Graduates*				
per 10 000 population	52	46	43	43
Higher education				
Total	460	477	433	401
In:				
day departments	289	300	237	216
evening departments	51	49	47	44
distance learning	120	128	149	141
Graduates*				
per 10 000 population	33	33	29	27

* Russian: *spetsialisty*.

Source: Nar. khoz. RSFSR 1990, s. 253.

Students* completing specialised secondary and higher education: by sectoral affiliation of their institution, 1980–90 (thousands)

	1980	*1985*	*1989*	*1990*
Specialised secondary education				
Total	721	659	640	637
Industry and construction	287	247	226	219
Agriculture	106	100	87	81
Transport and communications	63	56	49	48
Economics and law	95	92	86	84
Health care, physical culture and sport	86	81	92	102
Education	71	71	89	93
Art and cinematography	13	12	11	10
Higher education				
Total	460	477	433	401
Industry and construction	190	196	162	144
Agriculture	38	42	38	36
Transport and communications	26	27	21	19
Economics and law	40	41	38	38
Health care, physical culture and sport	33	34	32	28
Education	129	133	138	132
Art and cinematography	4	4	4	4

* Russian: *spetsialisty*.

Source: Nar. khoz. RSFSR 1990, s. 254.

Overview of educational and cultural facilities, 1991

At the start of the 1991/92 school year, there were 6.8 thousand schools with 3.9 million pupils where the teaching of subjects took place at greater depth, 306 grammar schools with 219 thousand pupils and 198 high schools with 115 thousand pupils. During the previous year the number of the first-mentioned schools had increased by 2.2 times, grammar schools by 3 and high schools by 2.5 times. By 1 December 1991 a total of 85 private schools had been registered; 6.7 thousand pupils were studying in them.

* * *

In the 519 higher educational establishments (VUZy) the number of students was 2.8 million. In the 2.6 thousand establishments for specialised secondary education the students numbered 2.2 million. By comparison with 1990 the numbers had declined by, respectively, 2 and 3 per cent. In 1991 VUZy graduated 406.8 thousand specialists for the national economy and the technical colleges graduated 623.2 thousand. The problem of finding jobs for graduates became markedly more difficult.

* * *

At the beginning of 1992 more than 8 million children were in pre-school establishments. That figure represented 64 per cent of the relevant age group, as against 66 per cent in 1990. This reduction is linked to the creation of the opportunity for a parent to look after children under the age of three at home without loss in respect of her work record, and the payment of benefit in respect of young children who do not attend a kindergarten.

* * *

A reduction in attendance at cinemas, theatres, museums and libraries continues to occur in the republic. The unsatisfactory technical condition of library buildings, the overburdening of book storage facilities and the absence of up-to-date equipment has a negative effect on the library service. Every third club and every sixth library is operating in buildings which either require capital works or are in a ruinous condition.

Source: *Sotsial'no-ekonomicheskoe polozhenie 1991*, s. 13.

Note on translation:

grammar school	*gimnaziya*
high school	*litsei*
technical college	*tekhnikum*

9 Life Expectancy, Morbidity and Mortality

Average expectation of life at birth, 1970–90 (in years)

	Total population	Men	Women
1970–71	68.9	63.2	73.6
1978–79	67.7	61.7	73.1
1979–80	67.5	61.5	73.0
1983–84	67.9	62.0	73.3
1984–85	68.1	62.3	73.3
1985–86	69.3	63.8	74.0
1986–87	70.1	64.9	74.6
1988	69.9	64.8	74.4
1989	69.6	64.2	74.5
1990	69.3	63.9	74.3

Sources: *Nar. khoz. RSFSR 1988*, s. 29; *Nar. khoz. RSFSR 1990*, s. 107.

Average expectation of life at birth for urban and rural population, 1979–89 (in years)

	Urban			Rural		
	All	Men	Women	All	Men	Women
1979–80	68.0	62.3	73.1	66.0	59.3	72.4
1987	70.4	65.4	74.5	69.1	63.2	74.5
1988	70.1	65.4	74.2	68.7	62.7	74.4
1989	69.9	64.8	74.5	68.5	62.6	74.2

Sources: *Naselenie SSSR 1988*, s. 495; *Demograficheskii ezhegodnik SSSR 1990*, s. 390.

Spatial variation in average expectation of life, around 1990

Average life expectancy among the numerically small peoples of the North is 46–50 years. According to data from Norwegian experts, in the town of Nikel' people live only 44 years on average.

The average expectation of life for men in rural areas is 62.6 years. It stands at less than 56 years in rural Tuva; less than 59 in Novgorod and Tula *oblasti*, and less than 60 in Tver', Irkutsk and Kamchatka *oblasti*.

Sources: Article by V. Konenenko in *Izvestiya*, 1992, 22 yanvarya, s. 1; *Vestnik statistiki*, 1991, 7, s. 22.

Average expectation of further years of life after reaching specified ages, 1970/71–1989

	15	30	60
Men			
1970–71	50.7	37.4	15.0
1979–80	48.9	35.8	14.3
1989	51.2	37.8	14.9
Women			
1970–71	60.6	46.3	19.6
1979–80	60.1	45.7	19.3
1989	61.1	46.7	19.7

Note: A reduction of only a half in the number of those dying each year from accidents, poisoning and trauma would extend the life expectancy of the population in Russia by two years on average. In the case of men there would be an increase of three years.

Source: *Vestnik statistiki*, 1991, 7, s. 22 and 76.

Cases of illness giving rise to temporary loss of work capacity, 1985–90 per 100 workers*

	1985	1989	1990
All cases	**111.09**	**111.54**	**109.67**
Illness of worker	76.78	76.16	79.24
includes:			
'Flu and colds	36.38	35.93	36.98
Accidents**	3.76	4.11	4.60
Diseases of:			
circulatory system	6.10	5.41	5.69
musculo-skeletal system	6.28	7.41	8.34
gastrointestinal tract	3.20	3.25	3.36
Complications of pregnancy			
and the postnatal period	2.22	2.30	2.20
Caring for sick persons	31.95	33.41	28.86
Sanatorium-health resort			
treatment, quarantine	0.66	0.52	0.42

* From a sample of enterprises.
** Excludes industrial accidents.

Source: *Nar. khoz. RSFSR 1990*, s. 265.

Industrial accidents, 1990

A total of 432 000 persons suffered industrial accidents in 1990. For 8400 of them, death resulted. The loss of working time due to accidents at work amounted to 10.2 million man-hours in 1990.

Source: *Nar. khoz. RSFSR 1990*, s. 273.

Days of temporary loss of work capacity arising from illness, 1985–90 per 100 workers*

	1985	*1989*	*1990*
Total	**1164.8**	**1227.7**	**1249.0**
Illness of worker	962.2	942.7	999.5
includes:			
'Flu and colds	281.8	277.4	296.8
Accidents**	84.6	90.1	100.2
Diseases of:			
circulatory system	101.7	90.5	95.1
musculo-skeletal system	87.4	99.6	114.0
gastrointestinal tract	58.1	57.8	60.4
Complications of pregnancy			
and the postnatal period	35.4	38.6	38.3
Caring for sick persons	190.7	274.9	240.9
Sanatorium-health resort			
treatment, quarantine	4.5	3.5	2.9

* From a sample of enterprises.
** Excludes industrial accidents.

Note: Shortcomings in the prevention of illness, and in the timeliness and quality of treatment, lead to loss of capacity for work among employees. In 1990, as a result of temporary loss of work capacity, a total of 2.3 million persons were absent from work each day in Russia.

Source: *Nar. khoz. RSFSR 1990*, s. 265.

Persons first declared invalids: by cause of invalidity, 1990

Key to columns: 1 Blue- and white-collar workers
                 2 Collective farmers
                 3 Blue- and white-collar workers
                 4 Collective farmers

	1	2	3	4
	thousands		per 10 000 workers	
All	**330**	**27**	**51.7**	**66.5**
Circulatory system	108	8	16.9	18.8
Neoplasms	68	5	10.6	11.4
Traumas	41	4	6.5	8.9
Nervous system*	20	2	3.2	5.7
Musculo-skeletal system	22	2	3.5	4.9
Respiratory organs	18	3	2.9	6.5
Digestive organs	9	0.7	1.3	1.7
Tuberculosis	7	1	1.2	2.4
Occupational diseases and poisoning	3	0.2	0.4	0.4
Psychiatric	12	0.8	1.9	1.9

* and the organs of sense.

Note: Amongst the persons who were first declared invalids in 1990 a total of 108 000 were under 45 years of age.

Source: *Nar. khoz. RSFSR 1990*, 274.

Patients suffering from malignant neoplasms, 1980–90

	1980	*1985*	*1990*
First diagnosed:			
thousands	321	355	391
per 100 000 population	231	247	265
Registered cases:			
thousands	1318	1546	1665
per 100 000 population	948	1074	1124

Source: *Nar. khoz. RSFSR 1990*, s. 267.

Patients first diagnosed as suffering from malignant neoplasms: by localisation, 1990

	Men	*Women*	*Men*	*Women*
	thousands		*per 100 000 popn*	
Total	**197.1**	**194.2**	**283.9**	**246.6**
Includes cancer of:				
lip, oral cavity,				
pharynx	13.4	3.4	19.3	4.3
oesophagus	6.6	2.7	9.5	3.5
stomach	32.5	25.8	46.8	32.7
rectum	7.5	9.8	10.8	12.5
larynx	7.5	0.4	10.8	0.5
trachea, bronchi, lungs	57.0	10.8	82.1	13.7
skin	15.6	24.9	22.5	31.6
mammary gland	0.2	31.1	0.3	39.5
uterus	—	24.3	—	30.8
lymphatic and				
haemopoietic tissue	8.9	8.1	12.8	10.3
prostate gland	5.6	—	8.1	—

Source: *Nar. khoz. RSFSR 1990*, s. 268.

Patients suffering from alcoholism and alcoholic psychosis, 1980–90 per 100 000 population

	First diagnosed	All cases registered
1980	244.0	1458.4
1985	265.4	1953.6
1986	241.8	1980.5
1987	223.4	2008.6
1988	198.5	1999.9
1989	190.6	1886.8
1990	152.0	1790.6

Source: *Nar. khoz. RSFSR 1990*, s. 269.

Patients suffering from drug addiction and toxicomania, 1980–90 per 100 000 population

	First diagnosed	All cases registered
1980	1.3	12.5
1985	2.1	11.4
1986	4.5	13.4
1987	8.1	17.8
1988	5.6	20.6
1989	5.5	22.0
1990	4.4	23.6

Note: In 1990 health care units had a total of 5.2 million psychiatric patients on their registers, of whom 2.7 million were suffering from alcoholism and drug addiction. The corresponding figure for 1985 was 2.8 million.

Sources: *Nar. khoz. RSFSR 1988*, s. 238; *Nar. khoz. RSFSR 1990*, s. 269–70.

Patients under observation for psychiatric illnesses, 1985–90

	1985	1987	1990
Patients first placed under observation:			
thousands	678.6	641.7	391.8
per 100 000 population	473.0	440.3	264.9
includes:			
psychosis and dementia of old age			
thousands	17.9	18.8	9.9
per 100 000 population	12.5	12.9	6.7
schizophrenia			
thousands	29.8	29.6	19.5
per 100 000 population	20.8	20.3	13.2
non-psychotic psychic disturbances			
thousands	185.0	161.6	74.0
per 100 000 population	130.0	110.8	50.0
mental retardation (oligophrenia)			
thousands	59.2	65.1	39.0
per 100 000 population	41.3	44.6	26.4

Note: The significant reduction since 1987 in the number of patients with the diagnosis of psychic disturbance is caused by the change in the criteria for placing patients under dispensary observation. That resulted in the recategorisation of patients who do not require active medical observation.

Source: *Nar. khoz. RSFSR 1990*, s. 270.

Patients suffering from active tuberculosis, 1980–90

	1980	1985	1990
Cases first diagnosed:			
thousands	65.6	64.6	50.6
per 100 000 population	47.3	45.1	34.2
incl. respiratory cases:			
thousands	58.2	58.9	45.9
per 100 000 population	42.0	41.1	31.0
Registered cases:			
thousands	356.6	317.0	279.1
per 100 000 population	256.5	220.2	188.3

Note: Out of the total number of patients in whom the diagnosis of active tuberculosis was first established, over 40 per cent are bacteria carriers. More than a third of all patients present with the disease in an already advanced state.

Source: *Nar. khoz. RSFSR 1990*, s. 271.

Registered cases of infectious diseases, first seven months of 1991 and 1992

	1991	1992	% increase
Diphtheria	792	1 554	96.0
Tuberculosis	21 343	23 210	9.0
Scabies	27 862	56 111	101.0
Pediculosis	145 456	165 405	14.0

Note: The sharp rise in cases of diptheria is causing anxiety; epidemiologists associate it with the dangerous practice of parents not allowing their children to be vaccinated.

Source: *AiF*, 1992, 36, s. 8.

Sexually transmitted diseases, 1990–2

A small decline has occurred in the number of patients suffering from gonorrhoea; there were 180 883 in 1990 and 175 020 in 1991. For the first half of 1992 the figure was 87 724. It is recognised, however, that many people will rely on self-medication.

There were 9873 cases of syphilis in 1991 and 7178 in the first half of 1992.

Source: *AiF*, 1992, 36, s. 8.

Deaths of men per 1000 population of specified age group, 1980–90

	1980–1	*1985–6*	*1989*	*1990*
All ages	**11.9**	**11.0**	**11.1**	**11.1**
0–4	6.5	6.0	4.8	4.4
5–9	0.8	0.7	0.7	0.7
10–14	0.7	0.6	0.6	0.6
15–19	1.8	1.4	1.5	1.6
20–24	3.2	2.5	2.6	2.6
25–29	4.3	3.0	3.3	3.3
30–34	5.4	3.9	4.0	4.3
35–39	7.9	5.0	5.2	5.6
40–44	9.8	8.1	7.1	7.7
45–49	13.7	10.7	11.0	11.7
50–54	17.9	16.2	15.2	16.1
55–59	24.7	22.7	22.6	23.5
60–64	35.5	32.8	32.6	34.2
65–69	48.8	48.0	45.3	46.7
70 and over	100.9	97.6	104.8	104.8

Source: *Nar. khoz. RSFSR 1990*, s. 103.

Deaths of women per 1000 population of specified age group, 1980–90

	1980–1	1985–6	1989	1990
All ages	**10.2**	**10.7**	**10.5**	**10.9**
0–4	4.9	4.4	3.5	3.2
5–9	0.5	0.4	0.4	0.4
10–14	0.4	0.3	0.3	0.3
15–19	0.6	0.5	0.6	0.6
20–24	0.8	0.6	0.7	0.7
25–29	1.0	0.8	0.8	0.8
30–34	1.3	1.1	1.0	1.1
35–39	2.1	1.6	1.5	1.5
40–44	2.8	2.6	2.3	2.4
45–49	4.4	3.6	3.6	3.8
50–54	6.2	5.9	5.2	5.4
55–59	9.3	8.8	8.4	8.6
60–64	14.4	13.8	13.2	13.5
65–69	22.1	22.7	21.6	22.0
70 and over	70.2	70.6	74.6	78.0

Source: *Nar. khoz. RSFSR 1990*, s. 103.

Main causes of death per 100 000 population, 1980–90

	1980	1984	1988	1990
All causes	**1099.5**	**1157.7**	**1067.9**	**1116.7**
Infectious and parasitic diseases	20.6	18.3	13.3	12.1
Neoplasms	163.5	174.3	187.0	191.8
Diseases of:				
circulatory system	579.5	635.0	611.5	617.4
respiratory organs	92.1	81.9	62.2	59.3
digestive organs	30.0	31.3	27.3	28.7
Accidents, poisoning and traumas	165.0	160.2	103.4	133.7

Source: *Ekonomika i zhizn'*, 1992, 12, s. 10.

Deaths from non-natural causes, 1990

Around 200 000 persons died from accidents, poisoning and traumas in Russia during 1990; that is 50 000 or a third more than in 1987. Over the last three years deaths from these causes have increased by one and a half times in Tuva, Yakutiya, Khabarovsk *krai*, and Smolensk, Astrakhan', Ul'yanovsk, Chelyabinsk, Kemerovo, Chita, Amur, Kamchatka and Sakhalin *oblasti*.

These worrying changes in the level of deaths from non-natural causes are closely associated with the crisis situation in which society finds itself; the number of murders has almost doubled during this period, accidental alcohol poisoning with a fatal outcome has risen by 35 per cent and suicide has increased by 15 per cent. Almost one in five persons who died in 1990 put an end to their life by suicide.

Source: *Vestnik statistiki*, 1991, 7, s. 22.

Deaths from road accidents, 1991

In 1991 alone more than 37 000 people were killed on the roads of Russia. Every tenth victim was a child. Efforts to reduce this terrible indicator of road traffic accidents have not been successful. Moreover, in recent years it has risen inexorably.

In a number of countries people are classified as having died from road traffic accidents if their death occurs within 30 days of the accident. In Russia the corresponding period is one week.

In Europe, out of every 100 casualties on the roads 2–3 people die, but in Russia the fatality rate has reached 14 per 100. The reasons for this include the absence of normal communications on the roads, delayed provision of medical care, and absence of capability to organise a normal evacuation of the victims. One in ten of those who die is a child and a large proportion of the injured are young people.

Source: Article by V. Yakov in *Izvestiya*, 1992, 21 yanvarya, s. 8.

Fires and deaths from fires, 1991

A total of 259 000 fires was recorded in the Russian Federation during the period January–October 1991. That was 4.6 per cent above the figure for the same period in the previous year. The number which occurred in urban areas was 181 100 (70 per cent).

Almost 59 per cent of fires ocurred in dwelling houses, outbuildings, summer houses and garden sheds. The main causes were: carelessness with fire – 41.5 per cent; breaking rules of installation and operation of electrical equipment and electrical appliances for home use – 22.3 per cent; children playing with fire – 12 per cent; breaking rules of installation and operation of stoves and heating fixtures – 7.3 per cent.

In the first ten months of 1991 the deaths of human beings from fires amounted to 5700. A total of 35 500 head of cattle perished.

Source: *Statisticheskii Press-byulleten'*, 1992, 1, s. 96.

Deaths of children under the age of 1 year per 10 000 live births (IMR), 1981–90

	1981	*1985*	*1990*
All causes	**215.4**	**207.2**	**174.0**
Deaths from:			
Infectious and parasitic diseases	33.4	24.0	13.4
Diseases of nervous system and sense organs	4.2	3.6	3.2
Diseases of respiratory organs	66.1	48.2	24.7
Diseases of digestive organs	3.5	2.1	1.1
Congenital abnormalities	32.5	36.7	37.0
Conditions arising in perinatal period	59.7	77.7	80.1
Accidents, poisoning and trauma	10.6	9.0	7.1

Source: *Nar. khoz. RSFSR 1990*, s. 107.

Note: The IMR data need to be adjusted upwards to be fully comparable with the figures for most developed countries.

Perinatal deaths,* 1989

	Total	*Stillbirths*	*Deaths in 1st week of life*
Absolute numbers	38 330	19 618	18 712
Per 1000 live births and stillbirths	17.58	9.00	8.58

* In period elapsing between the 28th week of pregnancy and the end of the first seven days of life.

Source: *Demograficheskii ezhegodnik SSSR 1990*, s. 388.

Deaths of children under the age of 1 year, by cause, 1989

	Absolute numbers	*Per 10 000 live births*
All causes	**39 030**	**178.0**
Infectious and parasitic diseases	3 301	15.1
of which:		
intestinal infections	1 455	6.7
sepsis	926	4.2
Diseases of endocrine system, digestive disorders, impairment of the metabolism and immunity	252	1.2
Diseases of nervous system and sense organs	869	4.0
of which: meningitis*	332	1.5
Diseases of respiratory organs	6 221	28.4
of which:		
acute pneumonia	4 051	18.5
influenza	255	1.2
Diseases of digestive organs	307	1.4
Congenital abnormalities	8 099	36.9
of which:		
spina bifida, hydrocephalus	805	3.7
anomalies of circulatory system	3 358	15.3
Conditions arising in perinatal period	17 045	77.7
of which:		
birth trauma	3 019	13.8
intrauterine hypoxia, asphyxia at birth	2 493	11.4
Accidents, murder and other external influences	1 609	7.3

* Except where where occurring in deaths from infectious and parasitic diseases.

Source: *Demograficheskii ezhegodnik SSSR 1990*, s. 492.

Suicide, 1980–90

Year	Thousands	Rate per 100 000 population
1980	47.9	34.5
1984	54.0	37.9
1985	44.6	31.0
1986	33.3	23.1
1987	33.9	23.2
1988	35.7	24.3
1989	38.0	25.7
1990	39.2	26.4

Note: The death rate from suicide is 8 per 100 000 population in Great Britain, 12 in the USA, 20 in the Federal Republic of Germany and Japan, and 23 in France. [Years not given. Ed.]

Sources: *Nar. khoz. RSFSR 1990*, s. 105; *Nar. khoz. SSSR 1990*, s. 92.

Suicide per 100 000 population of specified sex and age group, 1984 and 1990

	1984		1990	
	Men	*Women*	*Men*	*Women*
All ages	**65.6**	**14.2**	**43.9**	**11.1**
Under 20	8.8	2.0	6.6	1.7
20–24	53.9	7.7	33.8	6.8
25–29	80.2	9.2	49.5	6.8
30–39	88.7	13.2	61.4	8.6
40–49	117.4	21.0	69.6	12.5
50–59	116.9	22.8	69.9	16.1
60–69	81.7	24.3	63.9	20.1
70 and over	105.4	31.0	96.9	30.7

Note: The death rate from suicide is four times higher among men than among women; it is seven times higher among men than among women in the age group 25–39.

Source: *Nar. khoz. RSFSR 1990*, s. 105.

Overview of health and healthcare, 1991

As in the past, temporary loss of work capacity remains at a high level. Every year the loss of working time from this cause amounts to 650–700 million man-days, or 10 days per worker on average. The most frequent illnesses, as in the past, are influenza, colds, and diseases of the skeleto-muscular system. During 1991 an increase occurred in malignant neoplasms, diseases of the circulatory, endocrinological and skeleto-muscular systems, and diseases of the blood and haematopoietic tissue.

* * *

At 1 January 1992 the number of persons known to be infected with HIV amounted to 518, including 266 children. Of the latter, 14 had been born to mothers who were infected with HIV. There are 61 patients suffering from AIDS, of whom 45 are children. The number of patients who have died from AIDS is 45, including 33 children.

* * *

The difficulty of providing pharmaceutical products to the Russian health service became very much worse. The supply of medicines in 1991 was less than half of what had been requested. There was a cutback in production of many types of medicines, in particular analginum, nitroglycerine, papaverine, eupheline and klopheline.

Source: *Sotsial'no-ekonomicheskoe polozhenie 1991*, s. 13–4

* * *

In June 1992 it was reported that in Kalmykiya 'over a hundred children' were infected with the AIDS virus.

Source: *Nezavisimaya gazeta*, 1992, 24 iyunya, s. 1.

10 Welfare, Housing, the Environment and Political Parties

Homes and boarding schools for child orphans and children without parental protection, 1985–90 (end of year)

	1985	1987	1990
*Number of homes for infants**	283	280	265
Infants (in thousands)	21.9	20.8	18.5
*Number of homes for children***	565	565	564
Children (in thousands)	63.0	54.7	42.4
Number of boarding schools	134	187	161
Total of boarders (in thousands)	38.8	48.4	29.3
Number of boarding schools for mentally handicapped	n.a.	n.a.	142
Mentally handicapped boarders (in thousands)	n.a.	n.a.	21.7

* Apparently infants aged between 0 and 3 years.
** Apparently children aged between 4 and 16 years. [Ed.]

Note: In accordance with the decree of the RSFSR Soviet of Ministers of 18 November 1988 No. 475, children's homes of a family type have been created. At 1 January 1991, there were 280 homes of this type in operation; they cared for 1772 thousand children.

At the end of 1990, boarding schools for mentally and physically handicapped children were teaching 38.1 thousand orphans and children left without parental protection; children's homes cared for 37.7 thousand and infants' homes for 4.3 thousand. In boarding schools 33.3 thousand were being taught; out of that total, 27.4 thousand were in boarding schools for orphans and children left without parental protection. A total of 170.5 thousand children were in wardship and 128 thousand orphans and children left without parental protection were under adoption.

Source: *Narodnoe obrazovanie v RSFSR*, s. 97.

Places in homes for the elderly and invalids, 1980–90

	1980	1985	1989	1990
Number of places (in thousands)	236	247	262	263
Places for the aged and for adult invalids (in thousands)	202	211	224	225
Places for child invalids (in thousands)	34	36	38	38
Places per 10 000 population	17.0	17.2	17.7	17.7

Note: The network of residential homes for the aged and invalids is developing at a slow rate. At 1 January 1991 the list of persons unable to care for themselves who were waiting to be accommodated in these homes stood at 12 thousand.

Source: *Nar. khoz. RSFSR 1990*, s. 284.

* * *

Homes for infants are provided at 11 corrective work colonies. At about mid 1992 the number of children cared for in them was 430.

Source: *M.N.*, 1992, 35, s. 19.

Invalids from childhood under age 16 on registers of social security agencies, 1980–90

	Thousands	*Per 10 000 children*
1980	52.9	17
1985	90.1	26
1990	155.2	43

Note: The increase in the number of invalid children is linked to the spread of congenital diseases and also of illnesses and accidents among children which subsequently give rise to partial or total loss of capacity for work.

Source: *Nar. khoz. SSSR 1990*, s. 253.

Eligibility for the old-age pension

At present, old age pensions are paid to men from 60 and to women from 55 years. Blue- and white-collar workers employed in underground work, in hot workshops and also in other occupations with heavy and harmful working conditions receive their pension 5–10 years earlier. Those who have been employed in various mining jobs for not less than 25 years have the right to retire on pension irrespective of their age. A reduction in the pension age also extends to persons who have worked in the Far North, to mothers who have borne many children, war invalids and other groups in the population.

* * *

At the start of 1991 persons in the various categories of pensioner in the Russian Federation amounted to 212 per 1000 population.

Source: *Nar. khoz. SSSR 1990*, s. 76.

Persons receiving pensions, 1980–90 (at end of year)

	Total	Old Age	Invalidity	Loss of breadwinner
		(in millions)		
1980	28.3	19.5	3.5	3.9
1985	31.2	22.5	3.5	3.7
1986	31.8	23.2	3.5	3.5
1987	32.2	23.8	3.5	3.3
1988	32.6	24.6	3.5	2.9
1989	33.2	25.2	3.6	2.6
1990	33.8	25.7	3.5	2.8

Source: *Nar. khoz. RSFSR 1990*, s. 131.

Old age pensioners receiving a minimum pension, 1980–90 (at end of year)

	Millions	As % of all old age pensioners
1980	4.0	21
1985	3.5	16
1988	3.2	13
1989	6.8	27
1990	6.3	24

Source: *Nar. khoz. RSFSR 1990*, s. 131.

Distribution of urban population by type of dwelling, at census of 1989 (in thousands)

	Persons	*Families*
Total	**107 959.0**	**29 663.3**
Those who specified their type of dwelling	102 112.6*	28 871.8*
Those living in:		
individual house	12 344.3	3 566.3
part of individual house	2 639.3	746.1
separate flat	72 009.9	21 015.2
communal flat	7 898.9	2 232.8
hostel	7 220.3	1 311.3
other	591.9	134.7
private rented	933.6	243.1
Average area per person		
Total	15 m^2	
Living	9 m^2	

* The totals are less than the sum of the entries below. [Ed.]

Source: *Gorodskie poseleniya RSFSR*, s. 146–7.

Provision of piped water and sewerage systems, 1980–1990
(at end of year)

	1980	1985	1990
Population centres with piped water:			
towns	986	1 017	1 037
urban-type settlements	1 761	1 854	1 785
rural centres*	2 663	3 190	23 824
Population centres with sewerage systems:			
towns	858	924	987
urban-type settlements	1 124	1 266	1 350
rural centres*	801	952	5 184

* The 1990 figure includes rural population centres with piped water and sewerage systems which are the financial responsibilty of collective farms.

Source: *Sotsial'noe razvitie RSFSR 1990: Tom II*, s. 23.

Percentage of urban housing stock* equipped with specified utilities, 1980–90 (at end of year)

	1980	1985	1990
Piped water	90	92	94
Sewerage system	88	90	92
Central heating	88	90	92
Gas	75	73	72
Hot water supply	60	73	79
Bath	80	83	87
Flats with gas (millions)	28.6	33.0	37.1
in towns and urban-type settlements	20.1	23.2	26.2
in rural centres	8.5	9.8	10.9

* In state, public and cooperative ownership.

Source: *Sotsial'noe razvitie RSFSR 1990: Tom II*, s. 23.

Percentage of rural housing stock* equipped with specified utilities, 1980–90

	1980	1985	1990
Piped water	29	39	49
Sewerage system	22	29	37
Central heating	28	32	37
Bath/shower	19	24	32
Hot water supply	9	13	19
Gas	61	73	78

* In state, public and cooperative ownership.

Source: *Sotsial'noe razvitie RSFSR 1990: Tom II*, s. 24.

Rehousing in towns and urban-type settlements, 1986–90

	1986	1988	1990
	(in thousands)		
Families and single persons rehoused:	1214	1346	1158
from waiting list	1078	1212	1102
as % of those on list	15	15	12
Families and single persons on waiting list*	8037	8983	9456
as % of all families and single persons	23	25	26

* Citizens recognised as being in need of rehousing are those with a living space of 5–7 m^2.

Source: *Sotsial'noe razvitie RSFSR 1990: Tom II*, s. 7.

Overview of housing provision, around 1990

The total area of the housing stock in the RSFSR amounts to 2176 million square metres. Of that, 1660 million are located in towns and 516 million in the countryside. As regards ownership, the state owns 1440 million, cooperatives 90 million, public organisations 9 million and individuals 637 million square metres.

The average overall living area per person in the republic is $16.4\,m^2$. The lowest regional average is $11.9\,m^2$ (in Chita *oblast'*) and the highest is $19.8\,m^2$ (in Pskov *oblast'*). The corresponding figure for Moscow is $18\,m^2$. In the USA, Denmark, Germany and France the figures are: 60, 50, 42 and 30 m^2, respectively.

Nearly 30 million square metres of the housing stock are in a ruinous condition. Capital works need to be undertaken urgently in respect of 120 million and reconstruction in required for 80 million square metres.

The number of people living in communal flats in the Russian Federation is 5 425 500. The number of families on the waiting list for housing is 9 964 100. However, about 1.3 million families are housed each year (in 1990 the figure was 1 296 200 families).

Source: Ogonek, 1991, 38, s. 13–14, 17.

Privatisation of flats, 1991

In the territory of the Russian Federation during 1991 a total of 113 000 flats in state and public ownership were privatised. This represented an area of 5.6 million square metres and a value of 670 million roubles. The average size of a privatised flat was $49\,m^2$ and the average value was 5925 roubles.

Of the privatised flats about 10 000 were transferred without charge to the personal ownership of Russian citizens. The average size of a free flat was $54\,m^2$, the average approximate value being 7 962 roubles.

The number of privatised flats and the number of free transfers exceeded the figures for 1990 by 2.6 and 20 times, respectively.

As in the past, the privatisation of dwellings proceeded successfully in Krasnodar, Stavropol' and Altai *kraya*, and in Rostov, Omsk and Volgograd *oblasti*.

The process proceeded least satisfactorily in St. Petersburg, Ul'yanovsk, Amur, Sakhalin and Magadan *oblasti* and in the republic of Tuva (under 100 flats).

From the commencement of the policy in Russia, 167 000 flats have been sold or transferred into personal ownership. That constitutes an area of 8.1 million square metres, representing 0.5 per cent of the state and public housing stock. The total value of privatised dwelling amounted to 925 million roubles; the sum of 496 million roubles was realised from sales. About 68 per cent of all privatised flats were acquired by the population in 1991.

Sources: *Statisticheskii Press-byulleten'*, 1992, 1, s. 14; 2, s. 44–5.

Opinion on environmental changes near place of residence over previous five years, July 1990* (in percentages)

	Better	*Same*	*Worse*	*Don't know*
Drinking water	3.6	48.0	37.6	10.8
Food products	1.4	16.2	75.3	7.1
Air	1.6	22.5	65.0	10.9
Parks, squares, streets	6.5	28.7	51.1	13.7
Nearby woods	1.2	20.7	53.5	24.6
Reservoirs	1.4	15.5	64.9	18.2
Beaches and leisure spots	3.1	20.5	57.6	18.8

* Sample size: 56 000 persons.

Note: Those who were completely satisfied with the general condition of the environment near their place of residence amounted to 9 per cent of the interviewees; 74 per cent were dissatisfied and 17 per cent were undecided.

Source: *Nar. khoz. RSFSR 1990*, s. 311.

Polluted effluent discharged into natural reservoirs, 1985–90

Year	Million cubic metres
1985	11 981
1987	16 723
1989	27 146
1990	27 799

Note: The source seems to imply that the increase from 1987 is largely artifactual, reflecting a definitional change by the water protection agencies which are concerned to achieve higher standards of purification. [Ed.]

Source: *Vestnik statistiki*, 1991, 12, s. 59.

Noxious emissions into the atmosphere* in cities with the highest levels of environmental pollution, 1990 (thousand tonnes)

Key to columns: 2 Solids
                  3 Sulphur oxides

	Total	2	3
Angarsk	391.3	102.9	124.4
Arkhangel'sk	79.0	19.8	38.3
Barnaul	165.1	63.9	46.4
Berezniki	33.5	7.0	8.6
Volgograd	206.9	35.3	29.5
Volzhskii	57.0	2.7	9.2
Groznyi	238.3	6.1	19.6
Dzerzhinsk	96.7	9.8	38.9
Ekaterinburg (Sverdlovsk)	58.3	19.0	2.4
Zapolyarnyi	72.0	4.1	67.2
Zima	40.8	11.7	10.0

Kalinigrad	50.8	11.1	25.8
Kamensk-Ural'skii	72.2	33.7	11.5
Kemerovo	94.7	25.7	22.4
Komsomolsk-na-Amur	64.0	17.5	15.5
Krasnoyarsk	244.5	70.2	40.7
Lipetsk	643.1	50.0	40.9
Magnitogorsk	791.1	147.3	69.5
Monchegorsk	258.1	16.0	233.4
Moscow	273.8	23.4	51.9
Nizhnii Tagil	559.3	100.0	73.2
Novokuibyshevsk	243.1	1.9	47.4
Novokuznetsk	572.7	104.3	52.2
Novotroitsk	220.4	39.7	18.6
Noril'sk	2298.8	31.8	2201.7
Orsk	461.9	48.2	175.6
Omsk	438.8	109.0	160.2
Perm'	152.2	8.4	29.7
Prokop'evsk	41.3	15.0	5.6
Salavat	98.0	4.3	30.5
Samara	122.0	11.3	31.8
Sterlitamak	132.0	25.3	19.7
Tol'yatti	103.3	18.8	10.4
Ufa	260.3	7.1	48.5
Khabarovsk	141.1	47.0	45.6
Cherepovets	599.7	66.5	47.8
Chelyabinsk	391.5	102.6	46.3
Shelekhov	44.6	24.1	2.9
Yuzhno-Sakhalinsk	26.0	12.2	7.5

* From stationary sources.

Source: *Nar. khoz. RSFSR 1990*, s. 309.

Emissions of specified noxious gases into the atmosphere*
in cities with the highest levels of environmental pollution, 1990
(thousand tonnes)

Key to columns: 1 Carbon monoxide
2 Nitrous oxide
3 Hydrocarbons**

	1	2	3
Angarsk	46.1	26.6	69.3
Arkhangel'sk	12.1	7.3	0.3
Barnaul	23.2	19.3	3.2
Berezniki	12.2	3.6	0.0
Volgograd	52.9	18.3	20.1
Volzhskii	28.0	8.7	1.0
Groznyi	18.7	11.8	142.3
Dzerzhinsk	21.1	13.3	3.9
Ekaterinburg (Sverdlovsk)	16.9	11.9	0.7
Zapolyarnyi	0.4	0.3	—
Zima	0.9	4.4	0.1
Kalinigrad	9.1	2.2	0.0
Kamensk-Ural'skii	19.6	6.3	0.1
Kemerovo	11.9	27.4	0.3
Komsomolsk-na-Amur	8.5	8.4	12.3
Krasnoyarsk	108.7	12.7	0.3
Lipetsk	516.7	30.1	0.4
Magnitogorsk	526.7	32.4	5.8
Monchegorsk	1.4	5.1	0.6
Moscow	29.9	116.2	3.4
Nizhnii Tagil	353.6	25.5	0.5
Novokuibyshevsk	31.7	18.4	122.2
Novokuznetsk	366.5	38.8	1.4
Novotroitsk	144.7	14.6	0.7
Noril'sk	15.0	20.2	—
Orsk	186.5	11.3	36.3
Omsk	38.9	42.9	71.5
Perm'	17.8	22.1	2.8
Prokop'evsk	15.7	4.3	0.1

Salavat	12.0	16.0	28.2
Samara	23.3	17.4	1.7
Sterlitamak	51.0	19.2	3.7
Tol'yatti	19.5	39.3	0.7
Ufa	29.1	25.7	136.0
Khabarovsk	28.6	9.1	7.8
Cherepovets	444.8	35.8	1.2
Chelyabinsk	204.3	25.8	1.6
Shelekhov	16.2	0.5	0.0
Yuzhno-Sakhalinsk	2.1	3.8	0.3

* From stationary sources. ** Excluding floating organic compounds.
Note: The figures 0.0 indicate an insignificant quantity; the sign —
indicates that the phenomenon does not occur.
Source: *Nar. khoz. RSFSR 1990*, s. 309.

* * *

As a result of measures taken to protect the atmosphere and also
as a consequence of the slump in industrial production, the
amount of noxious substances discharged into the atmosphere
fell by 13 per cent over the years 1986–90. In 1990 the total
volume amounted to 34.1 million tonnes.
Source: *Nar. khoz. RSFSR 1990*, s. 307.

Environmental disaster areas
(from the report of an official statement released in January
1992)

In Russia, up to the present, only districts (*raiony*) which were
badly contaminated as a result of the Chernobyl catastrophe and
districts in the South Urals have been officially declared
environmental disaster zones. To these should be added several
areas in the Volga region, in Central Yakutiya, in the Amur
region, in Kranoyarsk *krai* and in the Kola peninsula. Practically
every republic, *krai* and *oblast'* could designate their own zones
of environmental danger or disaster.

Until now an aspect of environmental protection to which little attention has been paid is the increasing risk of technology-driven catastrophes (fractures in pipelines and earthquakes – for example, those caused by pumping large quantities of water from deep in the earth). For instance, in Russia up to 700 major oil and gas pipeline fractures occur each year. According to different estimates this causes the loss of 7–20 per cent of the total amount of oil extracted, in other words tens of millions of tonnes.

It is forecast that in twenty years' time the water table will be at dangerously high level in over half of the area of Moscow. Even at present an average of 10 000–15 000 roubles is expended per urban resident on the rescue of existing buildings in Russia.

The extent of contamination by radiation in Russia is not fully known. In all, over 120 nuclear explosions were conducted for so-called peaceful purposes. More than 20 took place in the Volga basin and 12 in Yakutiya. Only fragmentary information exists about the serious radioactive contamination of areas as a result of the production of nuclear weapons in 'closed' cities: Chelyabinsk – 6, Arzamas – 16, Krasnoyarsk – 45 and Tomsk – 7.

Furthermore, it is not known what is happening in the shallow waters of the Kara Sea where the nuclear reactor of the nuclear-powered ship *Lenin* lies buried (after being thrown into the water). The same is true in respect of other sites where nuclear waste is buried. In the Russian government budget for the current year about five billion roubles are allocated for the battle against contamination by radiation.

Source: Article by V. Kononenko in *Izvestiya*, 1992, 22 yanvarya s. 1.

Overview of environmental issues, 1991

In 1991 there were cases of high and extremely high levels of atmospheric pollution in the cities of Arkhangel'sk, Amursk, Volgograd, Noril'sk, Saratov, Gubakha, Bratsk, Volzhskii and Ust'-Ilimsk. On several days three successive concentrations of noxious substances in the atmosphere exceeded the permitted limit by ten times. The main culprits were enterprises of the metallurgical, petrochemical and woodworking industries.

* * *

As a consequence of the continuing discharge of polluted effluents from industrial enterprises, very severe harm was caused to the river Chusovaya in Sverdlovsk *oblast'*, the Nyudai in Murmansk *oblast'*, the Rudnaya in Primor'e *krai* and the Tom' in Kemerovo *oblast'*.

The direct discharge of solid waste from town sewerage systems was the cause of the complete lack of oxygen in the rivers Mias in Chelyabinsk *oblast'* and Iset' in Sverdlovsk *oblast'*.

* * *

In the territory of Russia in 1991 about 18 thousand forest fires occurred; they covered almost 700 thousand hectares of forest and destroyed 10 million cubic metres of timber. The largest fires were recorded in Yakut-Sakha SSR, Krasnoyarsk *krai*, and in Irkutsk, Magadan and Tyumen' *oblasti*.

* * *

In 1991 data concerning the inspection of tree-felling locations indicated that the procurement of timber in the republic is carried out with huge losses of raw material. In woodcutting areas 2.5 million cubic metres of timber were abandoned, and what was spoiled in the cutting amounted to 5.0 million cubic metres.

Source: *Sotsial'no-ekonomicheskoe polozhenie 1991*, s. 25.

MEMBERSHIP OF POLITICAL PARTIES

Date of registration	Name of party	Membership at time of registration
14-03-91	Democratic Party of Russia	28 608
	Social-democratic Party of the Russian Federation	5 089
	Republican Party of the Russian Federation	over 5 000
12-04-91	Peasants' Party of Russia (KPR)	2 143
06-06-91	Russian Christian Democratic Movement Party	6 027
18-09-91	People's Party of Free Russia	5 233
25-09-91	Russian Christian-democratic Party (RKhDP)	2 356
	People's Party of Russia	1 318
	Constitutional-democratic Party (Party of National Freedom)	2 079
04-11-91	Russian Bourgeois-democratic Party	1 771
19-11-91	Russian Party of democratic reform	637
21-11-91	Socialist Workers' Party	2 500
09-12-91	Russian Party of Free Labour	1 734
	Christian-democratic Alliance of Russia	1 395
09-01-92	Russian Communist Workers' Party (RKRP)	over 6 000
15-01-92	Conservative Party	1 399
	Party of Constitutional Democrats of the Russian Federation	660
	National-republican Party of Russia	5 037
23-01-92	European Liberal-democratic Party	5 890
17-02-92	Free Democratic Party of Russia	1 696
20-02-92	Political Party of 'The New Left'	115
10-03-92	Republican Humanitarian Party	139
12-03-92	Russian Social-liberal Party	348
19-03-92	Russian Party of Communists	over 2 900
25-06-92	Party of Economic Freedom	662

Note: this information was supplied by the Ministry of Justice's Department for the affairs of social and religious societies. Its spokesman stated that shortly before July 1992 the largest party, the Democratic Party of Russia, was reported to have a membership in excess of 100 000 persons. In addition to the 25 parties listed above, some with only a few hundred members were known to the Ministry but had not been registered by it.

Source: *AiF*, 1992, 24, s. 8.

It can be added that in June 1992 a new political block known as the Civil Alliance came into existence when three existing parties decided to amalgamate. They were: the Democratic Party of Russia, the People's Party of Free Russia, and the Renewal Alliance.

Source: *M.N.*, 1992, 26, s. 7; also in the corresponding English language version.

11 Crime

Number of recorded crimes, 1985–90 (thousands)

	1985	1988	1990
Total	**1416.9**	**1220.4**	**1839.5**
Embezzlement of state or public property	208.4	177.1	317.4
Pilfering of state or public property	50.9	28.3	34.3
Crimes against personal property includes:	388.7	428.6	779.2
Theft	319.1	359.5	648.5
Robbery with violence	46.4	49.5	95.3
Speculation	19.4	24.3	26.8
Fraud	14.8	19.8	19.8
Distillation of spirits at home*	48.9	7.1	2.9
Premeditated murder, attempted murder	12.2	10.6	15.6
Premeditated bodily harm**	64.8	49.3	61.2
Rape, attempted rape	12.9	11.6	15.0
Drug offences	15.8	9.5	16.3
Hooliganism	143.1	81.7	104.7
Traffic and driving offences	74.1	80.1	96.3
incl. those causing death	11.9	11.4	15.9

* From May 1987 persons found guilty under this head have been punished under the administrative code. ** Grievous and less grievous bodily harm.

Source: Nar. khoz. RSFSR 1990, s. 286.

Note on translation:

embezzlement	*khishcheniya*
pilfering	*melkie khishcheniya*
theft	*krazhi*
fraud	*obman pokupatelei i zakazchikov*
robbery with violence	*grabezh i razboi*

Number of recorded crimes in major territorial-administrative divisions per 100 000 population, 1985–90

	1985	*1988*	*1990*
Russian SFSR	**989**	**831**	**1240**
Northern region			
Karelian ASSR	1020	695	1478
Komi ASSR	1509	945	1358
Arkhangel'sk obl.	1056	822	1383
Vologda obl.	831	657	1134
Murmansk obl.	834	677	1071
North-west region			
St. Petersburg (Leningrad)	983	890	1144
Leningrad obl.	1436	1157	1624
Novgorod obl.	1159	923	1377
Pskov obl.	1120	948	1650
Central region			
Bryansk obl.	965	745	1063
Vladimir obl.	667	583	952
Ivanovo obl.	833	647	1016
Tver' (Kalinin) obl.	875	724	1182
Kaluga obl.	849	680	848
Kostroma obl.	870	617	953
Moscow city	502	433	669
Moscow obl.	715	565	789
Orel obl.	817	700	840
Ryazan' obl.	853	677	994
Smolensk obl.	949	794	1093
Tula obl.	985	721	1049
Yaroslavl' obl.	920	750	1397
Volgo-Vyatka region			
Mari ASSR	889	681	1189
Mordvin ASSR	803	712	1123
Chuvash ASSR	762	612	931

	1985	1988	1990
Volgo-Vyatka region (*cont.*)			
Nizhnii Novgorod (Gor'kii) obl.	666	636	1496
Kirov obl.	1003	729	982
Central Black-earth region			
Belgorod obl.	707	546	880
Voronezh obl.	818	667	901
Kursk obl.	510	590	740
Lipetsk obl.	889	667	821
Tambov obl.	900	772	990
Volga region			
Kalmyk ASSR	1182	935	1322
Tatar ASSR	810	776	1234
Astrakhan' obl.	942	810	1299
Volgograd obl.	780	767	1195
Samara (Kuibyshev) obl.	1003	787	1097
Penza obl.	754	595	767
Saratov obl.	760	742	1248
Ul'yanovsk obl.	866	612	966
North Caucasus region			
Dagestan ASSR	605	480	692
Kabardino-Balkar ASSR	1031	852	1030
North Osetiya ASSR	919	943	1183
Checheno-Ingush ASSR	547	404	448
Krasnodar krai	1087	912	1209
Stavropol' krai	1048	897	1181
Rostov obl.	828	807	1322
Ural' region			
Bashkir ASSR	707	539	698
Udmurt ASSR	1034	787	1128
Kurgan obl.	1146	1212	1621
Orenburg obl.	880	781	933
Perm' obl.	1228	927	1370
Sverdlovsk obl.	1186	1011	1501
Chelyabinsk obl.	1094	833	1119

West Siberia region

Altai krai	866	879	1132
Kemerovo obl.	1007	848	1283
Novosibirsk obl.	997	845	1554
Omsk obl.	901	761	1155
Tomsk obl.	1261	1177	1731
Tyumen' obl.	1259	1002	1683

East Siberia region

Buryat ASSR	1208	1049	1670
Tuva ASSR	1881	1870	3163
Krasnoyarsk krai	1240	1055	1518
Irkutsk obl.	1405	1303	1688
Chita obl.	1027	964	1403

Far East region

Yakut ASSR	963	890	1453
Primor'e krai	1348	1167	1990
Khabarovsk krai	1465	1272	1814
Amur obl.	887	813	1276
Kamchatka obl.	1170	984	1622
Magadan obl.	1170	994	1473
Sakhalin obl.	1144	927	1601
Kaliningrad obl.	900	762	1387

Source: Nar. khoz. RSFSR 1990, s. 288–9.

Persons found responsible for crimes; by sex and age group, 1988–90 (thousands)

	1988	*1989*	*1990*
Total	**834.7**	**847.6**	**897.3**
Men	695.3	725.8	774.6
Women	139.4	121.8	122.7
Age at commission of crime:			
14–15	38.6	45.7	47.7
16–17	91.6	104.4	105.5
18–24	181.1	184.5	189.5
25–29	155.6	156.4	162.6
30 and over	367.8	356.6	392.0

Source: *Nar. khoz. RSFSR 1990*, s. 294.

Persons convicted: by age group and key categories, 1985–90 (percentages)

	1985	*1987*	*1988*	*1990*
Age:				
14–17	9.3	10.3	12.7	14.7
18–24	23.0	21.5	23.6	22.9
25–29	20.3	20.6	21.5	20.3
30–49	39.5	37.8	36.0	36.4
50 plus	7.9	9.8	6.2	5.7
Women	13.5	15.6	10.1	8.5
Previous offenders	38.1	36.2	41.5	39.6
Unemployed	23.1	15.2	17.0	20.3

Source: *Nar. khoz. RSFSR 1990*, s. 295.

Number of persons sentenced by the courts, 1985–90 (thousands)

	1985	1988	1990
Total	**837.3**	**427.0**	**537.6**
Embezzlement of state or public property	120.3	502.0	72.5
Pilfering of state or public property	26.2	13.8	11.6
Crimes against personal property includes:	165.4	93.8	135.9
Theft	122.4	72.2	98.2
Robbery with violence	39.1	20.0	35.6
Speculation	9.4	7.2	7.3
Fraud	6.3	6.1	7.8
Distillation of spirits at home	1.3	2.2	2.2
Premeditated murder, attempted murder	12.0	6.9	10.3
Premeditated bodily harm*	25.9	15.2	22.3
Rape, attempted rape	14.9	10.5	14.2
Drug offences	11.5	6.5	7.0
Hooliganism	115.9	44.7	52.2
Traffic and driving offences causing death	16.1	10.5	13.8

* Grievous and less grievous.

Source: *Nar. khoz. RSFSR 1990*, s. 290.

Number of persons under age 30 sentenced by the courts, 1987–90
(thousands)

	1987	1989	1990
Total	**304.0**	**258.1**	**311.5**
Embezzlement of state or public property	37.0	32.7	42.4
includes theft	30.7	29.0	37.6
Pilfering of state or public property	7.0	3.6	4.0
Crimes against personal property includes:	79.1	83.5	102.4
Theft	60.4	60.4	72.7
Speculation	3.1	1.8	3.2
Distillation of spirits at home	6.1	0.3	0.2
Premeditated murder, attempted murder	3.1	3.2	3.9
Premeditated bodily harm*	6.3	7.3	8.3
Rape, attempted rape	10.1	9.5	11.9
Drug offences	9.1	3.7	5.0
Hooliganism	50.0	33.1	38.6
Traffic and driving offences	15.9	13.1	15.2

* Grievous and less grievous.

Note: In 1990 juveniles committed – or participated in – 165 000 crimes (the corresponding figure for 1989 was 160 000). Every sixth crime fell into the serious category. The re-offending rate among juveniles was 10 per cent. The number of juveniles who committed offences while under the influence of alcohol was 6 per cent higher than in 1989.

The most frequent crimes committed by young people were: theft of state, public and personal property, drug offences, hooliganism, assaults on the police, stealing firearms, ammunition and explosives.

Amongst those of working age who were not in employment or education at the time of committing a crime, every seventh person came into the 16–17 age group and every third into the 18–24 age group.

In 1990 the courts of the republic directed 10 200 persons under the age of 30 to have compulsory treatment for alcoholism. The corresponding figure in respect of drug addiction was 164 persons.

Source: *Nar. khoz. RSFSR 1990, s. 296.*

Number of persons detained for being drunk in public places, 1987–90 (thousands)

	1987	1989	1990
Detained in a drunken or very drunken condition	4482.3	4401.5	4214.5
incl. juveniles	43.1	49.5	56.6

Source: *Nar. khoz. RSFSR 1990, s. 297.*

Murders, 1980–90

Year	Thousands	Rate per 100 000 population
1980	17.8	12.9
1984	16.4	11.5
1985	14.9	10.4
1986	10.6	7.4
1987	11.3	7.8
1988	14.3	9.7
1989	18.5	12.5
1990	21.1	14.3

Note: In 1990 a total of 60 300 persons were murdered or committed suicide; this figure represents 30 per cent of all deaths from accidents, poisoning and trauma.

Source: *Nar. khoz. RSFSR 1990, s. 105.*

Number of persons sentenced by the courts in major territorial-administrative divisions, 1985–90

	1985	1988	1990
Russian SFSR	837 310	427 039	537 643
Northern region			
Karelian ASSR	5 113	2 677	3 926
Komi ASSR	11 031	4 808	5 806
Arkhangel'sk obl.	10 162	4 592	6 394
Vologda obl.	7 668	4 079	4 960
Murmansk obl.	5 982	2 847	3 891
North-west region			
St. Petersburg (Leningrad)	25 585	12 332	13 588
Leningrad obl.	12 595	6 171	7 111
Novgorod obl.	5 967	3 092	3 732
Pskov obl.	6 331	3 349	4 485
Central region			
Bryansk obl.	8 392	4 378	5 245
Vladimir obl.	7 127	4 691	6 317
Ivanovo obl.	6 839	3 058	4 938
Tver' (Kalinin) obl.	9 874	4 978	6 013
Kaluga obl.	5 428	3 445	4 072
Kostroma obl.	4 784	2 474	3 056
Moscow city	28 599	12 936	20 549
Moscow obl.	27 189	11 252	15 546
Orel obl.	4 590	2 721	2 978
Ryazan' obl.	6 770	3 406	4 221
Smolensk obl.	6 397	3 566	4 471
Tula obl.	11 516	5 399	5 937
Yaroslavl' obl.	8 982	3 907	5 447
Volgo-Vyatka region			
Mari ASSR	4 031	2 300	2 487
Mordvin ASSR	5 540	3 521	2 973

Chuvash ASSR	7 109	3 250	4 272
Nizhnii Novgorod (Gor'kii) obl.	18 741	9 549	13 339
Kirov obl.	10 566	5 137	6 842
Central Black-earth region			
Belgorod obl.	6 149	3 253	4 201
Voronezh obl.	12 155	6 970	9 618
Kursk obl.	5 587	3 797	4 640
Lipetsk obl.	7 660	3 647	4 651
Tambov obl.	8 266	4 362	5 451
Volga region			
Kalmyk ASSR	2 516	1 115	1 611
Tatar ASSR	18 144	10 479	12 570
Astrakhan' obl.	6 070	3 569	4 550
Volgograd obl.	12 975	7 268	8 402
Samara (Kuibyshev) obl.	19 983	10 073	13 445
Penza obl.	7 175	3 936	4 859
Saratov obl.	12 875	7 280	9 037
Ul'yanovsk obl.	6 245	3 178	4 502
North Caucasus region			
Dagestan ASSR	6 787	2 977	4 298
Kabardino-Balkar ASSR	3 489	3 067	3 049
North Osetiya ASSR	3 365	1 769	1 803
Checheno-Ingush ASSR	4 185	1 906	1 791
Krasnodar krai	33 342	14 645	17 735
Stavropol' krai	16 522	10 109	11 479
Rostov obl.	24 661	13 105	16 111
Ural' region			
Bashkir ASSR	19 544	9 066	10 572
Udmurt ASSR	9 204	4 761	6 220
Kurgan obl.	7 909	4 387	6 486
Orenburg obl.	11 702	7 893	8 692
Perm' obl.	22 883	12 536	16 814
Sverdlovsk obl.	30 752	17 834	19 402
Chelyabinsk obl.	22 684	8 613	14 371

	1985	1988	1990
West Siberia region			
Altai krai	16 819	9 509	12 029
Kemerovo obl.	20 939	11 249	12 617
Novosibirsk obl.	18 970	8 226	11 024
Omsk obl.	12 268	6 647	8 685
Tomsk obl.	7 877	3 944	4 515
Tyumen′ obl.	16 732	10 362	12 571
East Siberia region			
Buryat ASSR	7 577	3 926	5 460
Tuva ASSR	4 305	1 827	2 265
Krasnoyarsk krai	26 481	12 711	16 738
Irkutsk obl.	19 651	9 390	11 656
Chita obl.	9 149	4 595	5 741
Far East region			
Yakut ASSR	5 825	3 174	4 468
Primor′e krai	16 659	7 885	8 819
Khabarovsk krai	14 659	7 377	8 148
Amur obl.	6 035	3 039	3 687
Kamchatka obl.	3 452	1 310	1 467
Magadan obl.	3 640	1 435	1 806
Sakhalin obl.	5 447	2 398	3 478
Kaliningrad obl.	5 088	2 498	3 503

Source: *Nar. khoz. RSFSR 1990*, s. 291–3.

Overview of crime, 1991

In 1991 the number of recorded crimes reached 2.2 million, which was 18 per cent higher than the figure for 1990. Every second crime was not cleared up. Criminal acts increased practically everywhere, and especially in Omsk, Vladimir, Novgorod, Sakhalin, and Kostroma *oblasti* (by 1.3–1.5 times).

The rate of recorded crime stood at 1463 per 100 000 population. In Leningrad, Sakhalin, and Tomsk *oblasti* and in Primor'e and Khabarovsk *kraya* this indicator was 1.4–1.7 times higher than the average for Russia. In the republic of Tuva it exceeded the average by 2.2 times.

* * *

An increase occurred in crimes with a mercenary motive. The proportion of crimes relating to property constituted 67 per cent of the total as against 61 per cent in 1990. A significant increase occurred in theft of state and public property (1.5 times) and of personal property (1.3 times), including theft from flats (1.4 times). Embezzlement on a large and very large scale rose by 14 per cent.

* * *

A total of 71.7 thousand crimes against the person were committed (compared to 71.5 thousand in 1990). Recorded murders stood at 16.2 thousand, an increase of 4 per cent. Crimes involving the use of firearms numbered 4.6 thousand. There were 783 recorded cases of thefts of firearms and ammunition.

* * *

Involvement in criminal activity rose amongst juveniles. They committed – or participated in – over 173 thousand crimes, an increase of 5.5 per cent. Every sixth crime committed by adolescents came into the serious category.

* * *

During the year the number of persons found responsible for committing crimes was 959 thousand. Of that total 13 per cent were women and 17 per cent were juveniles. At the time of commtting the crime, every sixth person was neither employed nor in education.

Source: *Sotsial'no-ekonomicheskoe polozhenie 1991*, s. 25–6.

Evaluation of personal safety, 1991

	Total	Men	Women
(percentage of respondents)			
Experienced anxiety about their safety during day:			
at home	16.9	11.1	20.6
on the street	29.8	23.3	33.9
in public places	27.8	22.7	31.0
on public transport	32.1	24.2	37.7
Experienced anxiety about their safety in evening:			
at home	37.3	26.9	43.8
on the street	79.0	67.4	86.3
in public places	64.4	54.6	70.6
on public transport	70.0	56.5	78.4

Notes: A survey of 40 thousand residents of towns and urban-type settlements in 23 regions of the RSFSR which was undertaken by the government statistical service in June 1991 showed that the population was seriously concerned by the crime rate. More than 40 per cent of respondents said that they had serious fears of becoming the victim of thieves and violent robbers. The same proportion were afraid of finding themselves in a situation which would result in severe injury or death at the hands of criminals.

Fear of becoming a victim of crime is frequently grounded in personal experience. Thus every fifth respondent indicated that during the last 18 months they personally or members of their families had suffered material or psychological harm from the acts of criminals (theft or attempted theft of personal property, damage to property, hooliganism, robbery etc.). Only 6 per cent of respondents considered that the press, radio and television artificially add to the fears concerning the crime rate.

The work of the police force was considered satisfactory by 23 per cent of respondents and was rated unsatisfactory by 36 per cent. The rest of the sample did not indicate their attitude. Approximately the same evaluation was made of the work of the courts and the procuracy.

A large number of those interviewed (39 per cent) had formed views about corruption in the agencies of the Interior Ministry, their illegal links with criminals and the existence of other infringements of the law.

In all, the results of the enquiry point to the conclusion that the increase in crime is increasingly an independent and extremely serious factor in the deterioration of the moral-psychological condition of society.

Sources: *Statisticheskii Press-byulleten'*, 1992, 1, s. 43–4; *Sotsial'noe razvitie RSFSR 1990: Tom II*, s. 326.

Number of recorded crimes, first half of 1991 and 1992
(thousands)

	1991	*1992*
Murder	8 184	10 058
Embezzlement of state property on large and very large scale	3 432	3 255
Speculation	12 644	3 553
Bribe-taking	1 732	1 542
Forging coin and notes	69	129
Theft of:		
state or public property	172 769	257 761
personal property	370 746	528 430
incl. from flats	127 561	204 742
Robbery of:		
state or public property	2 287	4 456
personal property	42 894	64 849
Robbery with violence of:		
state or public property	442	1 074
personal property	8 040	12 003
Fraud relating to:		
state or public property	1 662	1 646
personal property	8 781	9 598

Source: *AiF*, 1992, 38–9, s. 12.

12 Public Opinion: August 1991–August 1992

AUGUST 1991

The coup which failed

During the night of 18–19 August 1991, a group of anti-democratic, hardline members of the Communist Party leadership made a bid to take over supreme power in the Soviet Union. Triggering this action was their hostility towards an impending Union treaty which would have given a very substantial degree of independence to the fifteen republics at the expense of the USSR's central government. President Mikhail Gorbachev, on holiday in the Crimea, rebuffed their demands and was consequently placed under house arrest.

Asserting that Gorbachev was unable to perform his duties for reasons of health, the conspirators invoked an article of the Soviet Constitution as legal sanction for the assumption of his powers by Gennadii Yanaev, Vice-President of the USSR. They declared a state of emergency, began to issue decrees and, to assist the consolidation of their position, had tanks ordered into central areas of Moscow. Eight individuals styled themselves the 'State Committee for the State of Emergency in the USSR' (hereafter the Emergency Committee).

From the start, Moscow-based opposition to the coup d'état was led by Boris Nikolaevich Yeltsin, democratically elected President of the Russian Federation, and hence legitimate head of government in Russia. Supported by People's Deputies (elected representatives), Yeltsin made the Russian parliament building the literal and symbolic centre of resistance. On the morning of Monday 19 unarmed crowds began to form outside it; they were joined by the crew of a few tanks. At one point

188

Yeltsin came out of the White House, climbed up onto one of the tanks and read out a statement which defiantly condemned the coup. Television carried this potent image around the world.

In his first address 'To the Russian people' Yeltsin castigated the Emergency Committee's actions as a 'right-wing, reactionary and anti-constitutional revolution'. He also called for an emergency Congress of Deputies of the USSR and appealed to Russian citizens to 'make a worthy reponse' to the coup leaders, demand the return of constitutional government, and embark on an general strike of indefinite duration.[1]

In that and subsequent official declarations, Yeltsin seems to have hoped to key into two powerful but basically separate forces. The first can be identified as the constellation of sentiments which would stand opposed to civil war in Russia. The second can be described as the determination of liberal democrats to preserve those institutional arrangements and a range of civil liberties which had only recently come into existence. In this connection it is relevant that the Emergency Committee quickly became known as the Junta.

The public's attitudes towards the profound political crisis which had been created were sampled on the following day (20 August) in four major centres of population. Early findings from the survey appeared in the first issue of the newspaper *Argumenty i fakty* to be published after the coup had collapsed within less than seventy hours of its inception.[2] The responses obtained in Leningrad (as it still was named), Voronezh in the south of Russia, Krasnoyarsk in Siberia, and the Ukrainian city of L'vov were as follows.

Question: **Do you think that the action of the Emergency Committee is legal?**

Cities Answers	Voronezh	Krasnoyarsk	Leningrad	L'vov (%)
Illegal	49	76	54	71
Legal	28	12	23	13
Undecided	23	12	23	16

Do you think that the advent to power of the Emergency Committee will lead to an improvement or a worsening of the economic situation in the country?

Cities	Voronezh	Krasnoyarsk	Leningrad	L'vov (%)
Improvement	24	9	19	12
Worsening	38	77	46	59
Undecided	38	14	35	29

Do you think that mass repressions could begin now?

Yes	57	61	71	62
No	26	23	19	21
Undecided	17	16	10	17

What is your attitude towards Yeltsin's call for an indefinite strike?

Support it	30	57	40	42
Don't support it	49	33	31	38
Undecided	21	10	29	20

As can be seen above, in all four cities substantial proportions of respondents either considered the action legal or had no opinion either way. However, the combined figures are far higher for Voronezh and Leningrad (roughly one half of respondents) than for Krasnoyarsk and L'vov (roughly one quarter). The fact that between 12 per cent and 23 per cent were undecided may be explained, in part, by reference to restrictions which the Emergency Committee attempted to impose on news conveyed by the mass media.

At a broader level of interpretation those findings can be taken to indicate that a substantial part of the population failed to express support for the principle of democratic government. Such a conclusion, however, needs to seen against Russia's unique historical fate: Tsarist autocracy followed by totalitarian rule under the Communist Party. In this connection it can be recalled that Stalin's unexampled tyranny had ended as recently as 1953, the year of his death. The process of liberalisation under Gorbachev was so recent that, understandably, the attitudes of very many ordinary people were still conditioned not by expectations common to mature pluralist democracies but by the 'inertia of fear'.

Answers to the second question may be said to have a bearing on the assertion that many Russians were prepared to trade food for the new political freedoms which Gorbachev's reforms had introduced. Certainly expectations of an improvement in the economy were highest in Voronezh and Leningrad, with figures which are close to the proportions who regarded the Emergency Committee's action as legal. All the same, there as elsewhere, the optimists were outnumbered by the pessimists.

Responses to the third question reveal widespread fear of political repression under the Emergency Committee. In each city over half of respondents said that they thought mass repressions could be imminent, and the figure rose as high as seven out of every ten in Leningrad. Incidentally, the phrase 'mass repressions' may well have had frightening historical associations for some people in the sample since it was in use to describe the Stalinist terror of the late 1930s.

Regarding attitudes towards Yeltsin's call for an indefinite strike, it can be seen that these differ substantially as between the four cities. The highest level of support occurred in Krasnoyarsk, the city which also contained the largest proportion of respondents who thought that the actions of the Emergency Committee were illegal.

Notes

1. E. Rasshivalova, N. Seregin (redaktory), *Putch: Khronika trevozhnykh dnei*, Moskva, Progress, 1991, s. 19–20. This address was signed not only by Yeltsin but also by Ivan Silaev, who held the post of Prime Minister of Russia, and by Ruslan Khasbulatov, Deputy Chairman of the Russian Supreme Soviet.

2. *AiF*, 1991, 33, s. 3. The poll was carried out by the Centre for Public Opinion and Market Research (hereafter VTsIOM) with the support of the Public Opinion Foundation. The number of people questioned is given as 1438 but possibly that figure includes residents of other cities whose responses were not included in the published table.

In the aftermath

Apart from Gennadii Yanaev, the formally recognised members of the Emergency Committee were as follows:

Vladimir Kryuchkov	Chairman of the KGB (Committee for State Security)
Marshal Dimitrii Yazov	Minister of Defence
Boris Pugo	Minister of the Interior
Valentin Pavlov	Prime Minister of the USSR
Oleg Baklanov	First Deputy Chairman of the Defence Council
Aleksandr Tiyazkov	President of the Association of state enterprises in building, transport and communications
Vasilii Starobudtsev	Chairman of the Farmers' Union of the USSR (i.e. heads of state and collective farms).

If Marshal Yazov had not been persuaded to join the conspiracy, the Emergency Committee could hardly have gone so far in their attempt to gain supreme power. However, in order to overcome the defiance of Yeltsin and the Russian Parliament, they also required the obedience of others who held senior positions in the command structure of the armed forces. Those individuals, in turn, required the loyalty of their troops.

In his address 'To the Russian people', Boris Yeltsin called on servicemen not to take part in 'the reactionary rebellion'. Later on the same day (19 August) he made an appeal specifically to soldiers and officers in which he urged them not to become tools in the hands of 'this group of adventurists' (the Emergency

Committee). Invoking the humanitarian imperative of avoiding civil bloodshed, he asked them to think of relatives, friends and the nation to which they had sworn an oath of allegiance.[1]

In a purely military sense capturing the White House by storm represented a feasible task; the troops assigned to carry it out were the 'Alpha' anti-terrorist unit of the KGB. Before the scheduled time of attack an exploratory tank advance took place – only to be aborted after meeting determined resistance from the unarmed crowd who continued to defend their parliament in defiance of a curfew. And as the hours passed, it became clear that the military commanders would not involve their troops in further action which was bound to cause much bloodshed. By early afternoon on Wednedsday (21 August), troops were being ordered back to barracks. Radio stations broadcast the news of their withdrawal from Moscow.

In the immediate aftermath of the failed coup, the weekly newspaper *Moskovskie novosti* commissioned an opinion poll which posed two questions about key actors in the preceding events.[2] The first concerns the role of the army. It will be seen that although almost half the respondents had not changed their views about the army as a result of its actions, three in every ten now had greater confidence in it. This can be construed as endorsement of the 'mutiny' which had proved crucial to the collapse of the coup attempt.

Question: **Has your confidence in the Soviet Army changed during the last few days?**

	%
It has not changed	49
It has increased	30
It has decreased	12
Undecided	9

The second question asked about the responsibility of the Communist Party, differentiating between its main component elements. As can be seen below, fewer than than one in ten people believed that the Party bore no blame for what had happened. That is hardly surprising for at least two reasons. First, all eight conspirators who formed the Emergency Committee were members of the CPSU. Second, during the attempted seizure of power no condemnation came from the highest level, namely the Party's Central Committee.

Question: **Do you think that the Communist Party bears responsibility for the actions of the Emergency Committee?**

	%
Only the leadership	32
The Party apparatus	32
The Party as a whole	19
The Party is not responsible	9
Undecided	8

Notes

1. Rasshivalova, Seregin (redaktory), *Putch: Khronika trevozhnykh dnei*, s. 46–7.
2. *M.N.*, 1991, 35, s. 2. Sample: 1155 persons in 14 cities of Russia were interviewed on 24–26 August. This and all subsequent polls reported from *M.N.* were undertaken for the newspaper by VTsIOM with the support of the Public Opinion Foundation.

Suspension of the Soviet Communist Party

Even in the immediate post-coup period, as was shown above, very many people took the view that the Communist Party had been implicated in the actions of the Emergency Committee. With the passage of time, they were able to gain a clearer picture of the extent and form of this complicity. For example, it emerged that the Party headquarters in Moscow had sent out advice to officials in the provinces on how to provide support for the coup.

After the failure of the forces of repression, a day of reckoning awaited the CPSU. That it had signed a letter of political suicide was suggested in one of the posters which appeared in Moscow during the momentous days of mid-August. 'After 19 August', the prophetic message ran, 'there is no CPSU in the country'.

On his return from the Crimea, President Gorbachev initially appeared unaware of the wider implications of what had occurred. He committed himself to reforming, and hence perpetuating the Party. However, next day (23 August) Boris Yeltsin signed an order which suspended its activities throughout Russia, pending juridical investigation of the Russian Communist Party's involvement in the coup attempt. Its offices in Moscow and Leningrad were officially sealed and documents taken away for examination. This happened to the accompaniment of anti-Party demonstrations.

The passing-bell continued to toll. Gorbachev distanced himself from the Party by resigning from the post of General Secretary. The USSR Supreme Soviet, in effect following the lead of the Russian President, voted to suspend the Party throughout the territory of the Union. This action, which had become virtually inevitable, was taken on 29 August, with 283 Deputies voting in favour, 29 against and 52 abstaining.[1]

At about this time a survey was carried out by VTsIOM in which Muscovites were asked their views about what the future held for the CPSU. Over half (55 per cent) said they agreed with the statement that the Communist epoch, which began with the 1917 Revolution, had now come to an end.[2]

Notes

1. *Keesing's Record of World Events*, 1991, p. 38372.
2. *M.N.* 1991, 52 (sic), s. 6. The sample size and precise date of the poll are not given.

SEPTEMBER 1991

Attitudes towards Gorbachev

As was pointed out above, the Emergency Committee were motivated, at least in part, by opposition to Gorbachev's proposed Union treaty. This, though reserving a role for all-

Union government, provided for the devolution of unprecedented powers to the constituent republics. This treaty was due to be signed on 20 August and one of the conspirators' objectives, as expressed in their first statement, was to defend the 'territorial integrity' of the USSR in what they saw as a situation of 'political, inter-ethnic and civil confrontation, chaos and anarchy'.[1] So it was deeply ironic that their actions had the reverse consequence, acting as a catalyst for the disintegration of the Union.

While the power struggle went on in Moscow, it was predictable enough that Estonia and Latvia should seize the opportunity to declare themselves independent sovereign states, following the example which Lithuania had set in March 1990. These three Baltic republics had formed part of the 'Red Empire' only since their annexation early in the Second World War, but within a few days declarations of independence were also adopted in the homelands of other ethnic groups which had stronger links with Russia. Amongst those, the closest in terms of language, culture and historical experience, are Belorussians and Ukrainians, also Slavic peoples.

In his address to the Supreme Soviet on 26 August, Gorbachev collaborated with the inevitable by accepting – in effect – the right of republics to secede from the USSR. By the end of August, the territorial integrity of the Union was being relegated to the history books.

The remarkable rapidity of this process, comparable to the collapse of a house of cards, must be linked to the fate of the Communist Party. For the CPSU had been the coordinating force behind the Union. Once it ceased to function there was no power which could compel the various nationalities to inhibit their drive to self-determination.

At a lower level of significance, the position of the Union's President was undermined also by various changes which occurred in the machinery of government. These included the replacement of the USSR Cabinet of Ministers (which had endorsed the coup) by an interim committee for the management of the economy. That it was headed by Ivan Silaev, Prime

Minister of the Russian Federation, can be seen as indicative of a process whereby the Russian government extruded Soviet authority. The symbolic culmination of this process occurred at the end of the year when the Russian tricolour replaced the Soviet flag in the Kremlin.

As the power of the Union's President began to slip away irretrievably, attitudes of the general public towards Gorbachev were sampled in a poll undertaken for *Moskovskie novosti* at the end of August and beginning of September.[2] It shows that two out of every five respondents had not changed their minds about him since the coup. However, that finding should not be interpreted as indicating approval for his policies which latterly had been generally unpopular (or very unpopular) with many ordinary people. It is striking that, for whatever reason, almost a quarter of respondents now had a higher opinion of him than before. However, they were outnumbered by those who held a less favourable view.

Question: **Has your attitude towards Gorbachev altered since the coup?**

	%
It has not changed	42
It has worsened	27
It has improved	24
Undecided	7

Replies to a second question, which concerned Gorbachev's future, provide a somewhat more sharply focused perspective on the President's diminished political standing. It is striking that one in two (exactly 50 per cent) of those interviewed thought that he should remain in office. The idea of a new election – favoured by one-third – is to be understood against the previous political arrangements. As General Secretary of the CPSU, Gorbachev, of course, had never submitted himself to the judgement of the people and he entered on his tenure of the post of executive President without calling an election.

However, this lack of political legitimacy was presumably seen as irrelevant by those who took the view that if events were bringing about the demise of the Union, there would be no place for a Union President. The fact that 13 per cent of respondents thought that his post was unnecessary can be construed as demonstrating awareness that the old order was now in a state of irreversible decay. Indeed, the unravelling of this state formation continued at a rapid pace; it formally ceased to exist on 21 December 1991.

Question: **Which of these opinions about the President of the USSR would you agree with?**

	%
He should remain	50
There should be a new election	33
The post is unnecessary	13
Undecided	4

Notes

1. Rasshivalova, Seregin (redaktory), *Putch: Khronika trevozhnykh dnei*, s. 9.
2. *M.N.*, 1991, 36, s. 1. Sample: 1071 persons in 12 Russian cities were interviewed on 30 August–1 September.

Increased optimism about the future

If the collapse of the Communist regime and its machinery of repression gave many people a great sense of hope for the future, the virtual power vacuum and economic chaos justified feelings of deep anxiety. The winter months were now approaching and with them the possibility of worse hardships than occurred as a rule.

In a country which should have been able to feed itself, the chronic shortages of food and the gross inefficiencies of food distribution had long been a terrible indictment of the regime and its policies. But the decay of the administrative-command system meant that the position deteriorated in the short term; food distribution was one of the most urgent tasks which the

interim committee for the management of the national economy
had to confront. Early in September the situation in Moscow
was deemed to justify the setting up of an emergency committee
to coordinate food supplies for the city.

At about that time a poll commissioned by *Moskovskie novosti*
sounded out the attitudes of Muscovites towards a future in
which they were likely to experience or witness considerable
economic and social discontinuities. The results show that a
substantial minority were less optimistic than they had been a
month earlier – at the start of August. The outlook of a third
remained unchanged. The key finding, however, is that the
largest group of respondents were now more hopeful.

Question: **When you compare your feelings at the start of August
to those of today, do you have more or less hope about the future?**

	%
More	46
The same	32
Less	15
Undecided	7

(*Source*: *M.N.*, 1991, 37, s. 1. Sample: 1981 persons in Moscow were
interviewed on 7 September.)

Memorials of the past regime

On 22 August the toppling of a statue in central Moscow formed
part of legislative and ideological attack on the Communist
Party. As founder of Lenin's secret police system, Feliks
Dzerzhinski was widely associated with the arbitrary repression
and terror for which the previous regime could now be
unreservedly condemned by a free people. The statue of 'iron
Feliks' outside the KGB headquarters (the notorious Lublyan-
ka) acted as a magnet to exultant democrats on the streets of
Moscow and it was torn down to the cheers of a crowd which
included Boris Yeltsin.

Soon the Moscow city soviet set up special commissions with a
remit to make recommendations about which monuments

should be removed and which should be allowed to remain. Many statues, it can be said, did not simply have an historical significance as commemorating leading Communists but, at a deeper level, were also totems in the 'civil religion' devised and imposed as an element in the totalitarianism of the Soviet state. That held true, most clearly, for the most famous and symbolically potent of all such monuments, namely Lenin's mausoleum in Red Square.

Lenin himself, it should be said, had wished to be buried beside his mother in the Volkov cemetery in St. Petersburg. When the victory of democracy made possible the final rejection of cults and rituals created by the Communist regime, the removal of Lenin's embalmed corpse would have ended the tangible assertion of the leader's immortality. Here it should be noted that, at the end of August, in a change which had immense symbolic significance for its rejection of the Communist past, the city of Leningrad became St. Petersburg once again. This reversion to the original name had been legitimised by the result of a pre-coup referendum.

In mid-September Muscovites were asked what should be done with the mausoleum if it was decided that Lenin's body should now be buried. This poll revealed that a fifth of respondents were opposed to its continued presence, while as many as two-thirds said that it should be retained. It can be added that up to the time of writing, the Moscow city soviet had taken no action in this matter, perhaps with the main intention of avoiding unnecessary social and political friction.

Question: **If Lenin's body is committed to the ground, what should be done with his mausoleum?**

	%
Leave it	66
Remove it	20
Undecided	14

(*Source: M.N.*, 1991, 39, s. 1. A total of 2302 persons in Moscow were interviewed on 14–15 September.)

* * *

The data given above can be usefully compared to the results of a separate survey undertaken at about the same time which posed the more general question: what should be done about the monuments to Lenin? The proportion of respondents who wanted to have them removed was 30.5 per cent, while those who wanted to keep them was about double at 61.5 per cent. (The residual is accounted for by the respondents who were undecided.) Roughly the same figures were recorded in respect of monuments to Dzerzhinski and Karl Marx.

Greater discrimination in response was possible for people living elsewhere in Russia who were asked about their attitude towards monuments to Lenin. Thus respondents outside Moscow could express themselves in favour of removing some but not all. And that is what the majority – 43.1 per cent – did. The proportion who wanted all the monuments left in place was 35.1 per cent, while 15.7 per cent wanted them all removed and 6.1 per cent had no opinion either way.

Residents of larger population centres tended to take a more proactive attitude. Exactly one quarter of respondents in cities wanted to remove all monuments. In small towns and in the countryside the corresponding figures were 11 and 14 per cent, respectively. Such evidence of political passivity or general conservatism was more likely to be found in the latter areas, with their lower proportions of students and intellectuals. (It would strain credulity to suggest that the aesthetic qualities of these artefacts were objectively superior or were more highly prized in the countryside.)

(*Source*: Article by G. Pashkov in *Kul'tura*, 1991, 5, s. 1. The poll was carried out by the survey organisation 'Mnenie'. The sample size and interviewing dates are not given.)

The 'autonomous' republics

Just before the end of August, chairmen of the Supreme Soviets of ten autonomous republics issued a statement which, in effect, was a declaration of loyalty. It referred to the Federation as 'a single and indivisible state, hallowed by centuries-old traditions and the glorious history of the single multinational family of our peoples'. They were ready to have a new Union treaty signed in the name of the Russian Federation.[1]

Among the republics which did not support that line a particularly obvious trouble spot was Tatarstan, the capital city of which is Kazan' on the river Volga. The titular nationality, a Turkic-speaking people whose religious affiliation is Sunni Moslem, accounted for roughly half of the republic's total population. Political independence had been declared a year earlier, on 30 August 1990, and it is striking that Boris Yeltsin conveyed his congratulations on the anniversary.[2] But however proper his action as a recognition of legitimate democratic aspirations, large numbers of his fellow countrymen in that area had reason to be anxious, if not fearful, about what the future held for them.

Drawing on the local press, *Argumenty i fakty* reported a poll which had been conducted towards the end of September in the city of Almetevsk, which is located in Tatarstan's oil-producing region. (Oil installations in the republic had been taken into local control by means of nationalisation.) In this poll respondents were asked to express their attitude towards the possible departure of Tatarstan from the structure of the RSFSR. The ethnic breakdown was: Russians – 48.8 per cent, Tatars – 45.6 per cent, and other nationalities – 5.6 per cent. Those in favour of independence accounted for 17 per cent, while two-thirds – 64 per cent – were against. Those who were undecided amounted to 19 per cent. It is revealing that the idea of Tatarstan leaving the Russian Federation was unpopular with as many as 41 per cent of the Tatars questioned. For whatever reason, 7 per cent of the Russians living there wished the republic to be 'absolutely sovereign'.[3]

Notes

1. *Izvestiya*, 1991 29 avgusta, s. 1.
2. *Izvestiya*, 1991 30 avgusta, s. 2.

3. *AiF*, 1991, 40, s. 2. Sample: 1000 persons in Almetevsk were interviewed on 21–22 September.

OCTOBER 1991

Confidence in the republic's government

Question: **Do you think that the government of Russia is capable in the near future of making decisive reforms which will lead the republic out of its crisis?**

	%
No	50
Yes	28
Undecided	22

(*Source*: *M.N.*, 1991, 41, s. 1. Sample: 1,071 persons in 15 cities of Russia were interviewed on 5–6 October.)

The edition of *Moskovskie novosti* which published those poll results also carried an article which refers to the polarisation of opinion as shown up by other surveys. One of the questions asked what was more important for overcoming the country's crisis – constructing a democratic civil society or strengthening the authority of the ruling power. Only a third of the population replied that a civil society was more important. The remainder preferred a strong ruling power (it did not matter what sort), or declined to answer. And so, the article points out, the idea that the crisis could be surmounted only within the framework of a democratic society is not one which commands majoritarian support.

(*Source*: L. Gordon, 'V ozhidanii shoka', *M.N.*, 1991, 41, s. 6.)

Fighting amongst the republics

Question: **How likely is it that, within the next decade, major armed conflicts will occur between some of the republics of the former Soviet Union?**

	%
Very likely	32
Likely	28
Unlikely	18
Undecided	16
Completely unlikely	6

(*Source*: *M.N.*, 1991, 42, s. 1. Sample: The only details given are that the interviewing was undertaken on 12–13 October.)

Opinions about Yeltsin and democracy

Question: **How do you appraise the results of B.N. Yeltsin's activity in his first hundred days in the post of President of the RSFSR?**

	%
Negatively; he should resign	16
There are no real results but Yeltsin is the only figure who is capable of holding this post	23
Positively; he must continue his work in the post	35
Undecided	26

Question: **In your opinion, what is more necessary for the country now: democracy or 'a strong hand'?**

	%
Democracy	51
'A strong hand'	35
Don't know	14

(*Source*: *AiF*, 1991, 41, s. 1. Sample: 1175 persons in towns of Russia, Ukraine and Belorussia were interviewed on 16 October by TsSEI 'Tinni-Sotsio'. In Ukraine and Belorussia, 13 per cent of respondents questioned did not answer the first question on the ground that: 'This is Russia's problem'.)

Should Yeltsin have emergency powers?

Question: **Would you approve or disapprove of giving Boris Yeltsin emergency powers for carrying out urgent economic reforms?**

	%
Approve	63
Disapprove	25
Undecided	12

(*Source*: *M.N.*, 1991, 43, s. 1. Sample: 1065 persons in 14 cities of Russia were interviewed on 16–20 October.

In the event, on the 28 October Yeltsin announced a package of radical reforms to 'kick-start' the Russian economy. (If necessary, he intended to proceed independently of other republics, eight of which had previously signed an economic agreement which would have gone some way towards adapting the USSR's supra-national structure to vastly changed circumstances.) At the same time he informed Parliament that he was asking for special powers to implement the programme. It soon became clear that he had in mind to introduce legislation by presidential decree, thus largely by-passing the legislature. After considerable debate, Parliament adopted Yeltsin's economic policies on 4 November. *Source*: Reports in *The Times*.

A question of identity

Question: **What nationality would you like to have?**

	%
Present nationality	79
Nationality of native population	4
American	3
French (especially women)	2
Finns	1
Jews	1
Germans	1
Refused to answer	9

(*Source*: *AiF*, 1991, No. 42, s. 1. Sample: 1236 adult persons in towns of Russia, Ukraine and Belorussia were interviewed on 23 October by TsSEI 'Tinni-Sotsio'.)

Goods and prices

The package of emergency measures which Yeltsin announced included one which had been long advocated as an essential element in a transition to a market-driven economy, namely the freeing of all prices which had been fixed by the state under the the rigid system of centralised 'administrative-command' planning. By this time prices for bread, meat, dairy products and many other goods and services were remote from the real costs of production. Indeed the previous failure of Gorbachev to take action in this matter can be identified as a major explantory factor in the economic deterioration over a period of some two years. As can be seen from the next survey, however, almost half of the respondents were opposed to the idea.

Question: **Do you support the introduction of free prices?**

	%
No	47
Yes	37
Undecided	16

(*Source*: *AiF*, 1991, 42, s. 1. Sample: 1236 persons in cities of Russia, Ukraine and Belorussia were interviewed on 23 October by TsSEI 'Tinni-Sotsio'.)

That the interviewing elicited a representative response is very largely confirmed by the results of another poll which was undertaken at around the same time. Every second respondent was in favour of retaining state prices.

Question: **They say that if prices are 'set free', goods and foodstuffs will appear in the shops. Are you for the introduction of free prices?**

	%
For state prices	50
For free prices	35
Undecided	15

(*Source*: *M.N.*, 1991, 44, s. 1. Sample: the interviewing took place in Moscow but the date and sample size are not given.)

NOVEMBER 1991

Penalties for local inaction

Question: **Would you agree or disagree with the view that local authorities should be punished most severely – even held criminally responsible – for non-execution of the orders and instructions of the President of the RSFSR?**

	%
Agree	77
Undecided	13
Disapprove	10

(*Source*: *M.N.*, 1991, 45, s. 1. Sample: 1070 persons in 14 cities of Russia were interviewed on 2–3 November.

Attitudes towards retrenchment

Question: **Relying on the success of radical economic reform by the Russian government, are you willing to 'tighten your belt' and for a year go without many things that you and your family were used to?**

	%
Yes	43
No	42
Undecided	15

(*Source*: *M.N.*, 1991, 46, s. 1. Sample: 1002 persons in 13 cities of Russia were interviewed on 9–10 November.

Will Russia split up?

Question: **Do you favour the unity of Russia or concession of the right to secede from it?**

	%
For unity	60
For the right of secession	28
Undecided	12

(*Source*: *M.N.*, 1991, 47, s. 1. Sample: 1002 persons in 13 cities of Russia were interviewed on 16–17 November.

Surging nationalism had been particularly evident in the Caucasian republic of Checheno-Ingushetiya. There the political leadership had been ousted in the immediate aftermath of the August coup attempt, which it had supported. Although representatives of the Ingush community wished to remain with the RSFSR, the Chechen National Congress movement seized power in a bid for independence from Russia.

Early in November Boris Yeltsin, in an attempt to reclaim authority, declared a state of emergency and despatched troops to the republic. They were surrounded by Chechen fighters and the potentially disastrous position was only redeemed by the decision of the Russian Supreme Soviet to annul the President's action.

This episode can be said to demonstrate that *force majeure* would not be employed to bring recalcitrant republics to heel, and the lesson was presumably not lost on secession-minded nationalists. On the other hand, ethnic Russian minorities in particular were bound to look to Moscow as the only source of power which could protect their interests. Some indication of how opinion had polarised was conveyed by the results of the poll reported above. The source gives no indication as to what proportion of respondents, if any, were resident in the homelands of ethnic minorities but it is striking that as many as 28 per cent of respondents favoured giving autonomous republics the right to secede from the Russian Federation.

* * *

A poll published early in the following month can be interpreted as giving evidence about the extent to which Russians felt themselves threatened as perceived colonists or aliens in the homelands of peoples with very different ethnic backgrounds from their own.

Question: **Should Russia protect the rights of Russians, or the rights of all citizens of Russia in equal measure irrespective of their nationality?**

	%
Rights of all citizens	73
Rights of Russians	23
Undecided	4

(*Source*: *M.N.*, 1991, 49, s. 1. Sample: no details are given.)

Attitudes to entrepreneurial risk-taking

Question: **Are you prepared to take out a bank loan in the near future in order to open your own business?**

	%
No	64
Yes	20
Undecided	16

(*Source*: *M.N.*, 1991, 48, s. 1. Sample: 1061 persons in in 14 cities of Russia were interviewed on 23–24 November.)

Elite opinion on the unity of Russia

Question: **What should be the principal position of the Russian leadership in relation to autonomous areas which insist on secession from the Russian Federation?**

	%
Recognise their right to secede	39
Act according to circumstances	26
Retain them by any means	12
Attempt to hold them by talks	9
Other answers	11
Undecided	3

(*Source*: *Sots. Is.*, 1992, 5, s. 157. Sample: 723 'leaders of opinion' were interviewed by telephone in November by the 'VP' Service for the Study of Public Opinion.)

DECEMBER 1991

An independent Ukraine

Question: **What are your feelings about the results of the referendum on Ukrainian independence?**

	%
Anxiety	58
Approval	20
Undecided	16
Have no knowlege of the matter	6

(*Source*: *M.N.*, 1991, 50, s. 2. Sample: 1060 persons in 13 cities of Russia were interviewed on 8–9 December.)

Would the Army support another coup?

Question: **Do you think that the army could act in support of a 'strong hand' strategy in the near future?**

	%
No	41
Yes	34
Undecided	25

(*Source*: M.N., 1991, 51, s. 1. Sample: 1005 persons in 14 cities of Russia were interviewed on 14–15 December.)

Looking back on 1991

Question: **What was the main event of the year?**

(responses are given in rank order)

	Russia	Ukraine	Central Asia Kazakhstan Azerbaidzhan
	Respondents in:		
Revolution attempt in August	1	3	1
'Free' prices	2	5	7
End of CPSU's activity	3	6	4
Choice of republic's president	4	2	5
Declaration of independence of republics	5	1	3
Referendum about maintaining USSR	6	7	11
Price rises in April	7	4	2
War in Persian Gulf	8	8	9
Exchange of 100 and 50 rouble notes	9	10	8
Conflict between Armenia and Azerbaidzhan	10	11	6
January events in Baltic states	11	9	10
Crisis in Checheno-Ingushetiya	12	13	12
Civil War in Yugoslavia	13	12	13
Novo-Ogarev Agreement	14	14	14

(*Source*: *M.N.*, 1991, 52, s. 6–7. Sample: 2075 persons in various republics of the former Soviet Union were interviewed in mid-December. Preliminary data.)

Fighting in Georgia

Question: **Do you agree or disagree with the Georgian opposition that overthrow of the president by means of armed force is permitted in the defence of democracy?**

	%
Disagree	54
Agree	25
Undecided	21

(*Source: M.N.*, 1992, 1, s. 2. Sample: 2040 persons in Moscow were interviewed on 28–29 December.

JANUARY 1992

The spectre of unemployment

Question: **Are you afraid that you may find yourself unemployed in 1992?**

	%
No	40
Yes	30
Non-working due to age	23
Undecided	5
Already unemployed	2

(*Source: M.N.*, 1992, 2, s. 2. Sample: 1009 persons in 13 cities of Russia were interviewed on 4–5 January.)

Loyalty to the government

Question: **If spontaneous mass actions against the Russian government start in your city or district, will you be amongst those who demonstrate against the government, or amongst those who demonstrate in its defence, or will you not get involved?**

	%
I will not get involved	42
Will be against the government	17
Will demonstrate in support of the government	16·
Such demonstrations are impossible	13
Undecided	12

(*Source*: *M.N.*, 1992, 3, s. 2. Sample: 1016 persons in 13 cities of Russia were interviewed on 11–12 January.)

Will monetary reform occur?

Question: **The Russian government assures us that there will be no monetary reform in the near future. Do you believe this or not?**

	%
No	62
Yes	20
Undecided	18

(*Source*: *M.N.*, 1992, 4, s. 2. Sample: 1070 persons in 14 cities of Russia were interviewed on 18–19 January.)

Strike action against price rises?

Question: **Do you support the calls for strikes against the increase in prices?**

	%
No	43
Yes	25
I am ready to take part	20
Undecided	12

(*Source*: *M.N.*, 1992, 5, s. 2. Sample: 1020 persons in 13 cities of Russia were interviewed on 25–26 January.

Views on Gorbachev

Question: **Do you approve of M.S. Gorbachev's decision to continue active involvement in politics after resigning [from the post of President of the USSR]?**

	%
Yes	43
No	41

(*Source*: *Sots. Is.*, 1992, 7, s. 153–4. Sample: 1000 persons were interviewed in Moscow in January by the 'VP' Service for the Study of Public Opinion.)

Is privatisation desirable?

Question: **Will the privatisation of dwellings improve your life?**

	%
No	40
Yes	25
In part yes, in part no	18
Undecided	17

Question: **Should the transfer to private ownership in Moscow be allowed for:**

(A) large industrial enterprises?

	%
Yes	44
No	38
Undecided	18

(B) public transport?

	%
Yes	41
No	43
Undecided	16

(C) hospitals, policlinics, other medical establishments?

	%
Yes	50
No	35
Undecided	15

(*Source: Sots. Is.*, 1992, 7, s. 154. Sample: 1000 persons were interviewed in Moscow in January by the 'VP' Service for the Study of Public Opinion.

FEBRUARY 1992

Responsiveness of government

Question: **What sort of supreme power, in your opinion, does Russia need at present?**

	%
One which takes notice of criticism from the press and political opposition	70
Undecided	21
One which does not tolerate any criticism of it	9

(*Source: M.N.*, 1992, 6, s. 2. Sample: 1048 persons in 13 cities of Russia were interviewed on 1–2 February.)

Is a peace-keeping force needed?

Question: **Today one can hear the view that it is necessary to bring in armed forces of the United Nations in order to resolve conflicts in the territory of the Commonwealth of Independent States. Do you agree with this view or not?**

	%
Disagree	46
Agree	31
Undecided	23

(*Source: M.N.*, 1992, 7, s. 2. Sample: 1061 persons in 13 cities of Russia were interviewed on 8–9 February.)

Assessing the Communist appeal

On the eve of the anniversary of the Bolshevik revolution, in an irony of history, President Yeltsin signed an order which banned the activities of the Russian Communist Party and the CPSU on Russian soil. It also required the dissolution of their organisational structures.

In taking that executive action, Yeltsin needed to circumvent the constitutional obstacle whereby political parties could only be banned by a decision of the courts. He did so by declaring that the events of 21–23 August clearly demonstrated that the CPSU had never been a party but 'a special mechanism for creating and exercising political power by means of commingling with state structures or by directly subordinating them to the CPSU'. Notwithstanding the suspension in late August, the Party's leadership had continued to take illegal action which was calculated 'to exacerbate the crisis and create conditions for a new revolution against the people'. While its organisational structures remained intact, there could be no guarantee that it would not attempt another coup or revolution.

Though relatively few in number, hardline Communists continued as a political force which constituted a threat to Yeltsin's government. Following the liberalisation of prices they were involved in protest demonstrations, the second of which occurred on 9 February. It was presumably in recognition of their growing challenge to the democratic administration that *Moskovskie novosti* commissioned a poll into public attitudes towards the former holders of monopoly power.

(*Source*:   *Vedomosti*, 1991, 45, s. 1799–1800; reports in *The Times*.)

Question: **Would you agree or disagree that the Communists should return to power in Russia?**

	%
Disagree	56
Agree, if they can resolve our problems	16
Don't care	15
Undecided	7
Agree	6

(*Source*: *M.N.*, 1992, 9, s. 2. Sample: 1105 persons in 13 cities of Russia were interviewed on on 22–23 February.)

The elite prefers Yeltsin

Question: **If it came to a straight contest for the leadership of Russia between Yeltsin, Rutskoi, and Khasbulatov, who would be your personal choice?**

	%
B. Yeltsin	53
A. Rutskoi	9
R. Khasbulatov	6
None of those	28

(*Source*: *Sots. Is.*, 1992, 7, s. 153. Sample: 613 'leaders of opinion' were interviewed btween 15 and 25 February by the 'VP' Service for the Study of Public Opinion.)

Six months after the failed coup

Early in March *Moskovskie novosti* carried an article which is particularly useful because it compares data from studies carried out by the All-Union Institute for the Study of Public Opinion (VTsIOM) and provides analytical commentary on the differences. This section both reports some of the findings and draws on the accompanying commentary written by the sociologist Yurii Levada.

The main table compares opinion about key political and economic issues in the USSR in mid-August of the previous year (before the coup attempt) and in Russia alone during mid-

February. Having drawn attention to a decline in the frequency of anxiety about price rises and scarcity of food and goods (which is surprising at first glance), Levada offers a conjectural but convincing interpretation. He suggests 'that reality has not proved so terrible as was expected (or that the forthcoming unpleasant price rises are not so frightful by comparison with those which have already occurred . . .)'.

While concern over ethnic conflicts increased, which is natural enough since they had intensified, a broad similarity of attitude emerges regarding another persisting issue: the weakness of the governing authorities. In comment Levada points out that although power is now exercised by different people in different structures, fundamentally much remains unchanged. The problems, the solutions found for them and the mistakes made have frequently remained the same. In consequence, 'it is not accidental that the parameters of public anxiety are also similar'.

Question: **Which of the domestic problems of our society cause you most worry?**

	August 1991	*February 1992*
	%	
Price rises	73	62
Scarcity of food and goods	64	50
Rise in crime	28	37
Threat of unemployment	19	22
Weakness of the authorities	19	21
State of the environment	17	15
Ethnic conflicts	14	22
Disintegration of the USSR	9	—
Disintegration of economic links	—	13
Threat of dictatorship	6	6
Departure from socialist ideals	4	3

(Sample size: August – 1954 persons in USSR; February – 1635 persons in Russia.)

* * *

The next set of tables looks at generalised public attitudes towards political and economic issues in January and February, respectively. As can be seen, all three reveal a modest shift towards a more positive or optimistic outlook. Levada makes the important point that this trend occurred in the month when hardline criticism of the government became more strident than at any time since the failed coup attempt.

Question: **What are your expectations of the political scene in Russia?**

	January	February
	%	
Changes for the better	18	27
Changes for the worse	61	56

Question: **What are your expectations of the economic scene in Russia?**

	%	
Changes for the better	15	22
Changes for the worse	72	68

Question: **How has your confidence in Russia's leadership changed in recent months?**

	%	
Increased	13	16
Declined	73	70

(Sample size: August – 1531; February – 1635. The figures for undecided repondents are not given.)

* * *

A comparison of responses to a question about the stock of foodstuffs at home in January and February, respectively, may help to explain the shift of opinion noted above; certainly it suggests that limited improvements occurred in an area of daily life which is likely to have a very direct impact on the general level of public satisfaction. As can be seen, a smaller proportion of respondents reported having certain items, but against that can be set various increases. Particularly sharp rises can be seen in the percentages of those who reported having sausage-type products, butter, eggs and fish.

Question: **Which of these do you have at home now?**

	January	February
	%	
Meat	57	64
Sausage-type products	20	79
Dairy products	48	66
Butter	39	66
Vegetable oil	63	33
Flour, cereals	78	42
Eggs	54	80
Fish	15	34
Potatoes	92	61
Vegetables	59	55

* * *

When discussing the notion of political restraint in a time of hardship, Levada makes a valuable observation about differences between two broad social groupings. 'Today', he writes, 'the chief support for popular confidence in the democratic authorities and their reformist undertakings are the best educated and most active strata of the urban population.' By contrast, current attempts by old-guard Communists and by right-wing xenophobic groups appealed to the least urbanised and least well educated.

Restraint is also seen as related to purposive action by individuals towards prudential objectives which they have set for themselves. A common finding which emerges from opinion polls, Levada states, is that a significant part of the population now counts on the new socio-economic order. Accepting the need for radical reform, these people are prepared also to endure the hardships which are entailed.

(*Source*:   Yu. Levada, 'Chto ostavil fevral'', *M.N.*, 1992, 10, s. 18–19.)

MARCH 1992

A new constitution for Russia

The draft of a new constitution, backed by President Yeltsin, was scheduled for debate in April at the Sixth Congress of People's Deputies of Russia. As the supreme legislative body for the country, only the Congress has the power to make changes to the written constitution. In that connection, therefore, it is a more significant instrument of government than the standing parliament (Supreme Soviet) in which Deputies also serve on an annual rotating basis.

Elected in 1990, the Deputies differed widely in their commitment to liberal-democratic reforms and it was expected that various groupings would display determined opposition to the draft constitution. For example, the Communists of Russia faction were known to have drawn up a rival document (which would obviously have had a strongly backward-looking character).

Early in March, Victor Sheinis, deputy chairman of the parliamentary committee responsible for drafting the official document, made a preemptive move aimed at defeating attempts to reject or modify it substantially. He warned that if Congress refused to pass the document the President would circumvent conservative opposition by arranging a nation-wide referendum.

As things turned out in April, Deputies decided not to consider alternatives to the official draft but demonstrated a very lukewarm attitude towards it. They had been given the choice of approving it as the basis for the new constitution, approving it in broad terms, or approving it only 'as the general conception for continued work'. They opted for the third, least positive motion.

(*Sources*:   Article by O. Bychkova in *Moscow News*, 1992, 12, p. 6; reports in *The Times*.)

Question: **What do you think will happen if the new constitution is not adopted by the Congress?**

	%
Undecided	33
It will increase the threat of a reaction	28
It will not matter	26
It will be correct	13

(*Source*: *M.N.*, 1992, 11, s. 2. Sample: 1038 persons in 13 cities of Russia were interviewed on 7–8 March.)

The illegal Congress

In a gesture of defiance directed against Yeltsin's government, a group of diehard Communists decided to reconvene the former Soviet Congress of Deputies in a special session. Epitomising the disaffection amongst a section of the military was an ex-General, Albert Makashov, who had commanded the Volga military region until his enforced retirement in the aftermath of the failed coup. Among the diehards' major political objectives were restoration of the Soviet Union, the Soviet Constitution and the powers of the former Soviet People's Deputies.

Scheduled to take place on 17 March, the anniversary of President Gorbachev's referendum on the unity of the Soviet Union, the calling of this Extraordinary Congress caused anxiety in the government. At a press conference one of Yeltsin's advisers, Sergei Shakhrai, used highly alarmist language, even evoking the spectre of civil war. He was reported as saying that in about half of all local authorities in Russia the leaders were the same as those who held power before the attempted coup; these men would interpret the success of the Congress as an encouragement to counter-revolution.

In fact, the whole episode passed off peacefully, and had some farcical aspects. Although the organisers had claimed that some 1400 former Deputies (out of a total of 2250) were interested in attending, it seems that only 200 turned up in Moscow for the Congress. Banned from the city, their meeting eventually took place at a hall in the village of Voronovo, with press reporters outnumbering Deputies. More important, no violence occurred on the evening of the same day, when only some 30 000 people took part in an associated rally in central Moscow. The size of the crowd was far less than the 100 000 or so which the organisers predicted.

(*Source*: AiF, 1992, 10, s. 2; reports in *The Times*.)

Question: **What will calling this Congress lead to?**

	%
To a deterioration	38
It will not matter	35
Undecided	17
To an improvement	10

(*Source*: M.N., 1992, 12, s. 2. Sample: 1058 persons in 13 cities of Russia were interviewed on 14–15 March.)

Making ends meet

Question: **If you have a problem of making ends meet at present, how do you propose to deal with this situation?**

	%
Find additional source of earnings	49
Economise on everything	24
Don't know what to do	14
Seek help	8
Have no such problem	5

(*Source*: M.N., 1992, 13, s. 2. Sample: 1000 persons in 12 cities of Russia were interviewed on 21–22 March.)

Will the Russian Federation disintegrate?

Question: **Do you think that Russia will maintain her present frontiers to the end of this year, or that several self-governing regions will leave, or that she will break up into several states?**

	%
Will maintain present frontiers	39
Self-governing regions will leave	24
Russia will break up	21
Undecided	16

(*Source*: *M.N.*, 1992, 14, s. 2. Sample: 1390 persons in Moscow were interviewed on 28–29 March.)

APRIL 1992

Popularity of recent governments

Question: **Which government do you think best serves (or served) the interests of the majority of the Russian people?**

	%
Undecided	53
Gaidar's	27
Ryzhkov's	12
Silaev's	5
Pavlov's	3

(*Source*: *M.N.*, 1992, 15, s. 2. Sample: 1054 persons in 13 cities of Russia were interviewed on 4–5 April.)

Attitudes towards government and Congress

Question: **Would you support a call for the government to resign because it is not coping with the tasks which confront it?**

	%
No	53
Yes	29
Undecided	18

(*Editor's Note*: Almost certainly, the above question was posed because Gaidar and his colleagues, in frustration at the opposition to their programme of policies, threatened to submit their collective resignation to President Yeltsin.)

Question: **Would you support a call for dissolution of the Congress?**

	%
No	44
Yes	36
Undecided	20

(*Source*: *M.N.*, 1992, 16, s. 2. Sample: 1924 persons in Moscow were interviewed on 8–9 April.)

Media and government

Question: **Do you think that criticisms of the Russian government on television, the radio and in newspapers should be greater, or less, or at the present level?**

	%
Greater	35
At present level	29
Less	21
Undecided	15

(*Source*: *M.N.*, 1992, 17, s. 2. Sample: 1029 persons in 13 Russian cities were interviewed on 18–19 April.)

Attitudes towards mixed marriages

Question: **From what nationalities would you not want to have a son-in-law or daughter-in-law?**

	%
Nationality does not matter	60
All except one's own	14
Peoples of the Caucasus	7
Negroes	5
Jews	3
Peoples of Central Asia	2
Others	3

(*Source*: *AiF*, 1992, 31, s. 5. Sample: 934 persons were interviewed in Moscow during April by the 'VP' Service for the Study of Public Opinion.)

The acquisition of firearms

Question: **Are you for or against people being free to acquire a firearm for their personal protection?**

	%
Against	44
For	43
Undecided	13

(*Source*: *M.N.*, 1992, 18, s. 2. Sample: 920 persons in Moscow were interviewed on 25–26 April.)

Question: **Do you want to have your own firearm?**

	%
Yes	53
No	41
Undecided	6

(*Note*: Although the question was not asked, 14 per cent volunteered the information that they already owned a firearm.)

(*Source*: *AiF*, 1991, 39, s. 1. Sample: size not specified. The polling was undertaken by TsSEI 'Tinni-Sotsio' in Moscow, St. Petersburg, Kiev and a further five unspecified cities on 2 September 1991.)

MAY 1992

A threatened strike

Question: **Do you support the Russian healthcare staff who have announced their intention to go on strike?**

	%
Yes	53
For	25
Undecided	12
I know nothing about it	10

(*Source*: *M.N.*, 1992, 19, s. 2. Sample: 1032 persons in 12 cities of Russia were interviewed on 2–3 May.)

The fact that a majority of respondents expressed support for healthcare staff, despite the potential dangers of a strike, may be explained in part by sympathy for the low rates of pay received by doctors and paramedics. It is also likely that attitudes were influenced by an awareness that a professed objective of the militant action was a higher level of public funding for health care, which would benefit patients. In the event, following an improved pay offer, the threat of an immedediate, country-wide strike was lifted.

Whose is the Crimea?

Question: **Do you think that Crimea should be part of Ukraine, or part of Russia, or be an independent state?**

	%
Part of Russia	66
An independent state	15
Undecided	12
Part of Ukraine	7

(*Source*: *M.N.*, 1992, 20, s. 2. Sample: 1051 persons in 13 cities of Russia were interviewed on 9–10 May.)

Attitudes Towards the Conspirators

Question: **Do you feel any sympathy for Kryuchkov, Yazov and other members of the Emergency Committee as persons in prison?**

	%
No	59
Yes	30
Undecided	11

(*Source*: *M.N.*, 1992, 21, s. 2. Sample: 1050 persons in 12 cities of Russia were interviewed on 16–17 May.)

Entrepreneurial activity

Question: **During the last six months, have you or a member of your family happened to sell any manufactured goods or foodstuffs on the street?**

	%
No	85
Yes	13
Yes, as my job	2

(*Source*: *M.N.*, 1992, 22, s. 2. Sample: 2219 persons in Moscow were interviewed on 23–24 May. The data were preliminary.)

Should the CPSU be put on trial?

Question: **Are you for or against a court trial of the CPSU?**

	%
For	50
Against – it is undemocratic	20
Don't care	12
Undecided	9
Against – CPSU supporters	9

(*Source*: *M.N.*, 1992, 23, s. 2. Sample: 1082 persons in 14 cities of Russia were interviewed on 30–31 May.)

A bad time to start a family

Question: **Do you agree with the view that now, when the future is so worrying and unclear, it is irresponsible to start a family?**

	%
No	52
Yes	38
Undecided	10

(*Source*: *AiF*, 1992, 18, s. 1. Sample: 1982 persons were interviewed by the 'VP' Service for the Study of Public Opinion. No further details are given.)

JUNE 1992

Disquiet about the future

Question: **When you think about your future, do you do so with feelings of confidence, hope, anxiety, or doom?**

	%
Anxiety	45
Hope	32
Doom	11
Confidence	6
Undecided	6

(*Source*: *M.N.*, 1992, 24, s. 2. Sample: 1003 persons in 13 cities of Russia were interviewed on 6–7 June.)

Land Ownership

Question: **Would you be for or against the introduction of the private ownership of land?**

	%
For	72
Against	16
Undecided	12

(*Source*: *M.N.*, 1992, 25, s. 2. Sample: 1037 persons in 13 cities of Russia were interviewed on 13–14 June.)

The Ostankino demonstration

Question: **Do the people who formed pickets near the Ostankino television centre in Moscow represent your personal interests?**

	%
No	54
Know nothing about it	19
Yes	14
Undecided	13

(*Source*: *M.N.*, 1992, 25, s. 2. Sample: 1082 persons in 13 cities of Russia were interviewed on 20–21 June.)

For ten days in June a TV Centre in Moscow was picketed by demonstrators who appear to have been predominantly ex-communists and extreme Russian nationalists. The protesters' basic objective was probably not so much to gain additional opportunities for their views to be disseminated as to put on a show of strength and intimidate the authorities. The situation acquired a tragi-comical character when the demogogue leader of the Workers of Russia Party, Viktor Anpilov, declared the area around the building unconquered territory of the revolution and himself head of a workers' and peasants' state. Early on the morning of 22 June, when a large rally was expected to converge on Ostankino, police dispersed the picket camp fairly rapidly but not without injuries. (*Sources*: Reports in *The Times*.)

Attitudes towards shareholding

'In keeping with the programme of privatisation, the Moscow city soviet is preparing to issue every Muscovite with a privatisation voucher. It will be possible to purchase company shares with it or to sell it'.

Question: **What will you do with this voucher: buy shares or sell it?**

	%
Buy shares	37
Undecided	34
Sell it	29

(*Source*: *M.N.*, 1992, 27, s. 2. Sample: 989 persons in Moscow were interviewed on 27–28 June. The data were provisional.)

Elite views on the CPSU

It should be noted that the following two questions were put not to a sample of the general public but to 500 persons who were deemed to be 'leaders of public opinion'. These included activists of political parties, directors of state enterprises, publicists, representatives of public organisations and executive authorities, and entrepreneurs.

Question: **Do you think that the adoption of Yeltsin's decrees 'Concerning suspending the activity of the Communist Party of the RSFSR' and 'Concerning the property of the CPSU and of the CP of the RSFSR' in August 1991 were necessary or were mistaken?**

	%
Necessary	55
Mistaken	30
Other opinions	10
Undecided	5

Question: **Do you think that it is necessary to pass a law which would prevent functionaries of the CPSU from holding leading posts in the structures of governmental power?**

	%
No	68
Yes	24
Other opinions	6
Undecided	2

(*Source*: Article by B. Grishin in *Nezavisimaya gazeta*, 1992, 21 iyunya, s. 2. The survey of 500 'leaders of public opinion' was carried out during June by the 'VP' Service for the Study of Public Opinion.)

JULY 1992

Electoral apathy

Question: **If elections were held now, would you vote for the supporters of Yeltsin, or for his opponents or would you abstain from voting?**

	%
For his supporters	35
Would abstain	35
Undecided	16
For his opponents	14

(*Source*: *M.N.*, 1992, 28, s. 2. Sample: 1305 persons in Moscow were interviewed on 4–5 July. The data were provisional.)

Alliance of extremists

Question: **What do you yourself think: is there a 'red-brown' threat or not?**

	%
Yes	42
No	37
Undecided	21

(*Source*: *M.N.*, 1992, 29, s. 2. Sample: 1305 persons in Moscow were interviewed on 4–5 July.)

This question concerns the danger to Russian democracy from an alliance between two groupings which, by convention, would be located at opposite ends of the political spectrum. The colours denote, on the one hand, die-hard Communists and, on the other, right wing ultra-nationalist and xenophobic organisations. Most notorious amongst the second category is Pamyat' (Memory).

Russia's world status

Question: **Do you agree with those who say that Russia should ensure that she remains a great power, even if this leads to a worsening of her relations with the surrounding world?**

	%
Agree	69
Disagree	20
Undecided	11

(*Source*: *M.N.*, 1992, 30, s. 2. Sample: 1707 persons in Moscow were interviewed on 14–15 July.)

Armed conflict with neighbouring states

Question: **How likely is it, do you think, that in the months ahead there will be armed conflicts between Russia and other republics of the former USSR?**

	%
Quite possible	44
Unlikely	39
Undecided	17

(*Source*: *M.N.*, 1992, 31, s. 2. Sample: 1703 persons in 13 regions of Russia were interviewed between 11 and 24 July.)

The danger of ultra-conservatism

Question: **Not long ago Boris Yeltsin spoke about forces which wish to reverse the progress of society. How probable is it that these forces can succeed in achieving their objective?**

	%
Improbable	47
Probable	30
Undecided	23

(*Source*: *M.N.*, 1992, 32, s. 2. Sample: 1707 persons in Moscow were interviewed between 27 and 30 July.)

Need for 'a strong hand'

Question: **There are people who consider that the only way out of the situation in which the country finds itself is the establishment of a strict dictatorship. Do you agree or disagree with this?**

	%
Disagree	41
Can't say definitely	32
Agree	27

(*Source*: *M.N.*, 1992, 33, s. 2. Sample: 1703 persons in 13 regions of Moscow were interviewed during July; dates not given).

AUGUST 1992

One year after the failed coup

Question: **What interpretation of events taking place since August 1991 would you most readily agree with: a renewal of the country has commenced; the crisis is deepening; a national catastrophe has occurred?**

	%
The crisis is deepening	47
A national catastrophe has occurred	24
Renewal has commenced	17
Undecided	12

(*Source*: *M.N.*, 1992, 34, s. 2. Sample: 1012 persons in 12 cities of Russia were interviewed on 11–12 August.)

Is the country being governed?

Question: **Do you consider that Russia's leadership controls the situation in the republic or that the situation has gone out of control?**

	%
The situation has gone out of control	56
The leadership controls the situation	24
Undecided	20

(*Source*: *M.N.*, 1992, 35, s. 2. Sample: 1695 persons 'in Russia' were interviewed between 8 and 18 August.)

Who is in charge now?

Question: **Who do you think is really in power in Russia at present?**

	%
Undecided	36
Reformers among the Communists	27
The former party apparatus	23
The new democrats	12
National-patriotic forces	2·

(*Source*: *M.N.*, 1992, 36, s. 2. Sample: 1695 persons 'in Russia' were interviewed between 8 and 18 August.)

Appendix I: Additional Notes

Blue- and white-collar workers and collective farm workers

As a rule, the above-mentioned are the three main socio-economic categories employed in the statistical sourcebooks which were produced under the Soviet regime. *Nar. khoz. RSFSR 1988* records that in 1988 their combined numbers amounted to 70.9 million, of which 45.5 million were classed as blue-collar workers (*rabochie*). There were 21.3 million white-collar workers (*sluzhashchie*) and 4.1 million collective farm workers (*kolkhozniki*) who were occupied in the farms' economic activity.

Censuses

Under the Soviet regime four major, Union-wide censuses were conducted in the post-war period. The dates of the census days are as follows:

1959	15 January
1970	15 January
1979	17 January
1989	12 January

In the preceding pages, unless otherwise stated, the figures given for those years will relate to the dates given above.

Unless otherwise stated, figures represent the *de facto* (*nalichnoe*) population, present on census dates, thus exluding persons who were temporarily absent, whether from the RSFSR or from territorial-administrative divisions within it. The figures relate to persons who were citizens of the USSR at the time of the censuses.

City/town

In Russian the word *gorod* denotes towns of all sizes, and thus includes even those with populations well in excess of a million, such as Moscow and St. Petersburg. I have chosen to employ the term *city* in contexts where a literal translation would appear inept.

Live births and the infant mortality rate

The Soviet definition of a live birth had the consequence of excluding a number of infants who were born with vital signs. This is evident from the statement: 'If a foetus is born alive but has a body weight of less than 1000 grammes, or is born before 28 weeks of gestation it is only counted as a live birth if it lives for a week (168 hours) from the moment of its birth' (I. S. Sluchanko, G. F. Tserkovnyi, *Statisticheskaya informatsiya v upravlenii uchrezhdeniyami zdravookhraneniya*, izdanie 2oe, Moskva, Meditsina, 1983, s. 50.

For that reason, let alone under-reporting of infant deaths, IMR data for republics of the former USSR require upward adjustment for the purposes of cross-national comparisons.

Marital status

The data for marriages and divorces relates only to those which have been officially registered by the relevant state agencies. Widows and widowers were previously in a state-registered marriage. The never-married are those persons who have not been in a state-registered marriage.

Urban/rural population

This categorisation is based on place of residence, as distinct from place of work. *Nar. khoz. RSFSR 1990* states that urban settlements are those centres of population which, under legislation, are counted as towns, urban-type settlements, and workers', health resort or summer house settlements. All other population centres are counted as rural.

In the early 1980s a centre of population in the RSFSR was classified as a town if it contained more than 12 000 persons, provided that over 85 per cent were blue- or white-collar employees and their families. It would normally be classified as an urban-type community if its population exceeded 3000, provided that over 85 per cent were blue- or white-collar employees and their families.

Appendix II:
Transliteration Table

Russian Cyrillic alphabet   *Latin alphabet*

А	а		A	a
Б	б		B	b
В	в		V	v
Г	г		G	g
Д	д		D	d
Е	е		E	e
Ж	ж		Zh	zh
З	з		Z	z
И	и		I	i
	й	(postvocalic)		i
К	к		K	k
Л	л		L	l
М	м		M	m
Н	н		N	n
О	о		O	o
П	п		P	p
Р	р		R	r
С	с		S	s
Т	т		T	t
У	у		U	u
Ф	ф		F	f
Х	х		Kh	kh
Ц	ц		Ts	ts
Ч	ч		Ch	ch
Ш	ш		Sh	sh
Щ	щ		Shch	shch
	ъ	(hard sign to indicate non-palatisation of preceding consonant)	"	
Ы	ы		Y	y
	ь	(soft sign to indicate palatisation of preceding consonant)		'
Э	э		E	e
Ю	ю		Yu	yu
Я	я		Ya	ya

Russian Cyrillic alphabet   *Latin alphabet*

Three adjectival-type endings

-его   -evo
-ий   -ii
-ый   -yi

Appendix III: Abbreviated Titles and Bibliographical Details of Sources

Journals and newspapers

AiF
Argumenty i fakty

M.N.
Moskovskie novosti

Sots. Is.
Sotsiologicheskie issledovaniya

Vedomosti
Vedomosti S"ezda narodnykh deputatov Rossiiskoi Federatsii i Verkhovnovo Soveta Rossiiskoi Federatsii

Books

Chislennost' naseleniya RSFSR
Gosudarstvennyi komitet po statistike (hereafter Goskomstat) RSFSR, *Chislennost' naseleniya RSFSR po dannym vsesoyuznoi perepisi naseleniya 1989 goda*, Moskva, Respublikanskii informatsionno-izdatel'skii tsentr, 1991.

Demograficheskii ezhegodnik SSSR 1990
Goskomstat SSSR, *Demograficheskii ezhegodnik SSSR: 1990*, Moskva, 'Finansy i statistika', 1990.

Gorodskie poseleniya RSFSR
Goskomstat RSFSR, *Gorodskie poseleniya RSFSR po dannym vsesoyuznoi perepisi naseleniya 1989 goda*, Moskva, Respublikanskii informatsionno-izdatel'skii tsentr, 1991.

Kratkaya kharakteristika naseleniya RSFSR, Chast' I
Goskomstat RSFSR, *Kratkaya sotsial'no-demograficheskaya kharak-teristika naseleniya RSFSR, (po dannym Vsesoyuznoi perepisi naseleniya 1989 goda), Chast' I*, Moskva, Respublikanskii informatsionno-izdatel'skii tsentr, 1991.

Kratkii statisticheskii byulleten' 1991
Goskomstat RSFSR, *Kratkii statisticheskii byulleten' za 1991 god*, Moskva, Respublikanskii informatsionno-izdatel'skii tsentr, 1992.

Nar. khoz. RSFSR for specified years
Goskomstat RSFSR, *Narodnoe khozyaistvo RSFSR: statisticheskii ezhegodnik*, Moskva. The yearbook for 1988 was published in 1989 by 'Finansy i statistika', and the yearbooks for 1989 and 1990 were published in 1990 and 1991, respectively, by Respublikanskii infor-matsionno-izdatel'skii tsentr.

Nar. khoz. SSSR 1990
Goskomstat SSSR, *Narodnoe khozyaistvo SSSR v 1990 g.: statisticheskii ezhegodnik*, Moskva, 'Finansy i statistika', 1991.

Narodnoe obrazovanie v RSFSR
Goskomstat SSSR, *Narodnoe obrazovanie i kul'tura v RSFSR*, Moskva, Respublikanskii informatsionno-izdatel'skii tsentr, 1991.

Naselenie SSSR for specified years
Goskomstat SSSR, *Naselenie SSSR: statisticheskii sbornik*, Moskva, 'Finansy i statistika'. The volume for 1987 was published in 1988 and the volume for 1988 in 1989.

Sotsial'noe razvitie RSFSR 1990
Goskomstat RSFSR, *Sotsial'noe razvitie i uroven' zhizni naseleniya RSFSR*, Moskva, Respublikanskii informatsionno-izdatel'skii tsentr, 1991 (two volumes).

Sotsial'noe razvitie SSSR 1990
Goskomstat SSSR, *Sotsial'noe razvitie SSSR 1990: statisticheskii sbornik*, Moskva, 'Finansy i statistika', 1990.

Sotsial'no-ekonomicheskoe polozhenie 1991
Goskomstat RSFSR, *Sotsial'no-ekonomicheskoe polozhenie Rossiiskoi Federatsii v 1991 godu*, Moskva, Respublikanskii informatsionno-izdatel'skii tsentr, 1992.

Statisticheskii Press-byulleten′ (numbers 1 and 2)
Goskomstat Rossiskoi Federatsii, *Statisticheskii Press-byulleten′*,
Moskva, Respublikanskii informatsionno-izdatel′skii tsentr, 1992.

Vozrast naseleniya SSSR
Goskomstat SSSR, *Vozrast i sostoyanie v brake naseleniya SSSR*,
Moskva, 'Finansy i statistika', 1991.

Zhenshchiny v SSSR 1991
Goskomstat SSSR, *Zhenshchiny v SSSR 1991: statisticheskie materialy*,
Moskva, 'Finansy i statistika', 1991.

Index